Coming Back to Learning

A Handbook for Adults

Tessa Doe, Helen Evans, Hilary Jones
and Debbie Steel

with
Sarah Marten

Lifetime Careers

Coming Back to Learning – 2nd edition

This edition revised 2004

Published by Lifetime Careers Publishing, 7 Ascot Court, White Horse Business Park, Trowbridge BA14 0XA

ISBN: 1 902876 88 1

Printed and bound by Cromwell Press, Trowbridge

Cover design by Jane Norman

Cartoons by Mark Cripps

Contents

Acknowledgements

We would like to thank Sarah Marten for her work in finding people willing to tell their stories for our profiles, and also the organisations which helped her in establishing contacts. Special thanks go to all those individual adult learners who have shared their experiences with us.

Our acknowledgements also to Paul Stirner, the author of *Coming Back to Education, 1994*, which still provides the basis for this book.

Introduction

Just to inspire you ...

'Returning to study has been an absolute joy, and has really improved my feelings of self-worth. Studying has brought meaning and a greater purpose to my life which will benefit both myself and, hopefully, others in the future.'

More and more adults are returning to study or training – some through necessity, as their knowledge and skills become outdated, some through an ambition to improve their prospects, and some for personal challenge and enjoyment. We are in an age of lifelong learning. Over 77% of students in further education colleges and 51% of entrants to higher education are over 21. Concerns among employers about skills shortages led the Government to set targets for learning, to be achieved by 2002. These targets were for 50% of adults (in or seeking employment and aged between 18 and retirement age) to have qualifications at level 3 (that's two A levels or equivalent) and 28% to be qualified to level 4 (HND- or degree-level). In fact, these targets were passed a year early.

Various government initiatives – such as the learndirect helpline, learndirect centres, adult learning grants, and the extension of Apprenticeships to adults – are intended to encourage more adults back into learning – although there are concerns about lack of funding for areas such as part-time higher education, adult residential colleges and other non-vocational learning.

How to use this book

This book is designed to help you to find the course of study or training that is right for you. It also provides practical advice on how to cope with any difficulties you may encounter once you have made your choice. There are plenty of resources and agencies out there to help you.

Adult education centres, colleges, universities, learndirect centres and numerous independent education and training organisations all offer opportunities for learning suitable for adults. Many of these are especially designed to fit around busy adult lives.

If you find attending classes regularly difficult, or just off-putting, there are plenty of alternative ways to learn. Flexible, open and distance-learning provision – including e-learning – allow you to study at your own pace, in your own time, at work, at college or at home. So, whatever your reasons for returning to education or training, you should be able to find something to suit you.

If you need encouragement to come back to learning, take a look at the profiles we have included in this book. They describe the personal experiences of people who have taken the plunge. Some have sailed through their course of study or training with no problems, others have faced difficulties, but all are positive about the benefits they have accrued – whether social, career-related or academic. Improved self-confidence and self-image are often mentioned.

The profiles are:

- **Wayne Barnes** – a full-time performing arts student at an FE college – chapter one

- **James Bawn** – to university via Australia – chapter five

- **Craig Brown** – knew he was good at English, and now has a qualification to prove it – chapter two

- **Carole Dyer** – from dental nursing to doctorate – chapter eight

- **Richard Griffiths** – a government-funded learner – chapter four

- **Richard Haines** – became a computer wizard through learndirect – chapter six

- **Janice Lawrence** – a 'return to learn' student – chapter three

- **Dermot Moorehead** – learning for pleasure, with students the age of his granddaughter! – chapter seven

- **Sacha Morris** – retrained as a hospital play specialist with the support of her family – chapter eight

- **Janet Namusoke** – first administration and now pattern-cutting – designing her own career path – chapter five

- **Rhonda Reid** – an Access course led to acceptance on to a degree course – chapter two

- **Jessica Sewell** – a false start resulted in a prison sentence, but she's using her time to study and has discovered a passion for knowledge – chapter one

- **Sandra Small** – returning to teaching – chapter seven

- **Arthur Smith** – from butchery to accountancy via college – chapter nine

- **Gary Smyth** – embarking on a degree course in nursing – chapter three

- **Emma Thew** – finding her future through history – chapter four

- **Sarah Valentine** – reaching for the stars (literally!) with the Open University – chapter four.

Despite their satisfactory outcomes, many of the people featured in these profiles did have doubts and concerns before embarking on their courses. You should find answers to whatever doubts and concerns you may have within the chapters of this book.

- Need to justify your desire to learn? You'll find good reasons in chapter one.

- Not sure about current qualifications? See chapter three.

- What options are available? Chapters two and four will explain, and chapter six will help you to choose.

- Worried about costs? Turn to chapter five.

- Don't know what to do with the kids? Try chapter seven.

- Where will it all lead? See chapter eight.

- Still don't know where to start? Chapter nine might be a good place.

Within each chapter, you will find sources of further information on the topics covered.

Correcting some misconceptions

Despite the trend of more adults returning to education and training, there are still some misconceptions around.

'You can't teach an old dog new tricks'

Few adults drop out of study or training because they find it difficult to learn. On the contrary, college and university teachers and lecturers will tell you that adult learners are usually more motivated and more committed than their younger colleagues. Consequently they often do better.

> 'At first as I was very rusty, but once I got into the swing of things all my educational skills started to return to me, sometimes in full flow.'

> 'Learning the second time around was, surprisingly, a lot easier. I think that I was actually ready to learn.'

'You can't get into higher education without A levels'

Entry into higher education is a lot more flexible than it used to be, even for school- and college-leavers. Where adult entrants are concerned, admissions tutors have always looked for evidence of ability to study to the required level, rather than specific academic qualifications. This is not because of a lowering of standards, but because they know that many people coming back to education, with no previous formal academic qualifications, have been successful students on all kinds of courses, including degrees.

> *'After getting a few GCSEs, I went to a local college to do a BTEC first diploma in engineering, but to be honest, I enjoyed the social life more than the course … I wasn't exactly what you'd call a motivated student!… Now [ten years later], I've just graduated with a 2:1 …'*

> *'The fact that my O levels were unspectacular didn't count against me, and all the things I felt were just something that I'd done because I had to – holding down a job whilst bringing up a child with my husband away in the forces, etc – turned out to be very creditable 'life skills'.'*

'You'll be the only one there over 25'

Colleges and universities have always opened their doors to people of all ages. Many go out of their way to attract mature students, and current policies to widen access to education and training mean they are rewarded for doing so!

> *'… you look around the classroom and see that the ages range from sixteen to seventy. If you look at their faces they look more scared than you feel!'*

'It won't help you to get a job'

Not only are employers demanding higher qualifications, but there are also increasingly strong links between education, training and industry. Many courses – such as foundation degrees – are directly work-related. Some are linked to particular employers. There are opportunities for gaining work experience on placements during some courses, which can even lead to job offers. National Vocational Qualifications place greater emphasis on practical ability, with assessment in the workplace based on demonstrating competence and skill rather than passing theoretical exams.

> *'Developing computer skills has enhanced both my job prospects and my creativity.'*

'It'll ruin your personal and family life'

A return to learning – especially full-time – can be difficult without the support of friends, partners and family. But many people find their lives and their relationships enriched by the experience.

> *'My son is highly amused to be doing his homework alongside his Dad…'*

Do some networking

Talking to people who have been there before will quickly demolish many of the myths that surround education. In particular, they will tell you not to be easily discouraged and not to underestimate your abilities.

… and remember

> *'… with determination and a bit of courage anyone can do it!'*

Chapter one
Why learn?

Reasons, reasons

'I decided to go back to learning when I realised that my CV had far too many gaps…'

'My mother's death made me think about my future.'

'I've always wanted to go into teaching, but I didn't think I'd have a chance because I don't have the right skills or the right qualifications.'

'I wanted to prove to people that I wasn't a doughnut.'

'As a parent, you want the best for your child and want them to achieve all their goals – and I thought why shouldn't I want the same for myself!'

'I knew if I was going to get back into the job market I'd need to know how to use a computer.'

'I told the rest of the class "I was here only for the fun".'

'Life's too short!!'

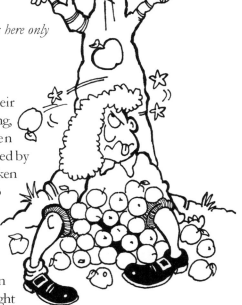

Ask a dozen adults to give their reasons for returning to learning, and you may get a dozen different answers – as illustrated by the quotes above, which are taken from profiles contributed to this book by a range of adult learners. What you can be sure of is that each of the adults that you question will be able to give you an immediate, yet carefully thought through, response. That's because they will have taken time to reflect upon their motivation, before their return to learning. Often, that decision is only arrived at after lengthy consultation with a range of people – friends, family, work colleagues, guidance professionals and tutors.

The responses to 'why learn?' are so varied because people return to learning from very different starting points. Perhaps your reason for considering a return to learning fits into one of these categories:

- for interest and enjoyment

- to improve and, often, prove yourself

- to gain qualifications that may raise your job and salary prospects

- to prepare for a return to work after a break.

Who are the adult learners?

There is no typical adult learner. All sorts of people take up learning again, often some time after leaving formal education. If you think about your circle of acquaintances, you almost certainly know people who go to adult part-time study or leisure classes. Or you may know someone who has retrained to take up a career they always dreamed of, but were diverted from while juggling home and family commitments with an unsatisfying job.

- Some young adult learners are fairly recent entrants to the labour market, who now realise they want to improve their qualifications and job prospects.

- Many learners need to upgrade their basic skills in reading, writing and numeracy – often as a precursor to further learning.

- Others are taking a proactive approach to advancing their career through broadening their skills and gaining additional qualifications.

- Many women (and some men), who held jobs with limited prospects and training opportunities before having a family, now need to reskill and improve their employability.

- A large number have reached a crossroads (or even a dead end) in their career path and seek a change of direction – perhaps leading to more interesting and satisfying employment – for the next stage of their working life.

- An equally large number of adult learners simply want to develop new interests or re-engage with old ones.

Do we ever stop learning?

We would probably all agree that learning is not a stop-start activity. We continue to learn from the challenges of every new situation, but, as adults, we don't necessarily recognise when we have acquired new skills or knowledge. We need to appreciate this in ourselves before we can expect others to acknowledge what we have learned!

We often feel there is no time to allocate specifically to study or to follow pursuits that are not essential to our jobs or our family life. If we are coping well and with confidence, why return to learning? It may take a change in our work or domestic situation to prompt us into undertaking a more formal and structured learning experience.

We like to know

Everybody enjoys feeling that they are abreast of things – that they are up-to-date with the news, gossip or sports results, and are aware of popular books, films, music, TV programmes, travel ideas and lifestyle choices. Nobody likes to feel like a stranger in their own culture. So how different is this familiarisation with new things from learning? It is fun to be up-to-date with TV soaps, and, as a result, we may learn ways of handling our own life choices from considering the issues tackled in *EastEnders* or *Coronation Street*.

We usually find it easy to remember information highly significant to ourselves. For instance, sports enthusiasts have very accurate recall of facts and figures connected with the teams they support, and not many people forget their own birthday! All this seems to indicate that, if you really want to learn – with whatever aim in mind – then you can learn.

So, what's in it for you?

If learning is the accumulation of knowledge and skills, we never opt out, although we can be quite unaware that the circumference of our knowledge is widening. Only gradually may it dawn on us that we have a fair grasp of a concept that we had not heard of a year or so ago. Think of digital cameras and shopping on-line! So, what are the reasons for taking up learning in a more proactive way? There are as many different reasons for taking up studying as there are people returning to learning. The profiles featured throughout the text are highly personal and emphasise the fact that everyone has a different start point from which they decide that learning is going to be a positive experience for them.

Wayne Barnes – decided to take action

Wayne returned to learning at the age of 39 to follow a course leading to a National Award in performing arts (acting).

'To begin with I found the experience of returning to full-time education quite daunting. At first as I was very rusty, but once I got into the swing of things all my educational skills started to return to me, sometimes in full flow. Being a mature student has helped me, particularly with learning to multi-task in full-time education. I have really enjoyed the interaction with all the people that I have met on this course and at the college. I found the help and support from all my tutors and other students invaluable. I feel that the experience that I have gained from my fellow students, both younger and older, very valuable. This is what helped me to excel at such speed, as I had thought my age would put me at a disadvantage.

My mother's death made me think about my future and this made me realise that, unless I furthered my studies, I had no real chance of a decent future. I decided to take action by applying for this course.

I would give anyone the advice that you should return to studies and, no matter what, get on with your learning rather than push yourself away in the corner and think you're not capable enough to complete or accomplish anything. Research the course that you're interested in and make sure that it's the right one for you. Look where the course might lead you in terms of career or job prospects, and how long your studies will last. Always keep in mind why you're doing the course and that only you can hold yourself back. Once you've decided, go for it and apply.'

In the following sections, the broad reasons for coming back to learning –

● fun and social engagement

● self-satisfaction and reward

● academic progress from any position – baseline to postgraduate

● to gain the vocational skills that employers seek

– are explored in more detail.

Learning for fun and social reasons

Increasing your own knowledge about a subject or topic that interests you is fun, and the mental exercise can be rewarding in its own right. Your enjoyment of life can be given a boost through:

● using your spare time or leisure in a positive way

● brushing up your skills, or learning to do something rather better than before

● facing a new challenge – trying something that you have never done before

● adding to your pre-existing knowledge base

● finding out the unexpected.

There is an important social aspect to taking up learning. Whether learning is approached in a formal or informal way, it is usually pleasant – and can be great fun – to meet people with the same or similar interests. These interactions – based on a shared interest – can be supportive and help to improve your self-confidence and your ability to talk about aspects of your learning. You may widen your circle of friends.

'As all the students were mostly in the same position it was easy to bond with everyone in the group and friendships were made very quickly. We are a very close group and all very supportive of each other.'

This social context of learning can be particularly strong in settings where the learning is non-vocational and is approached through community education classes, residential leisure courses, summer schools, adult education offered by further education colleges or in the extra-mural classes run by higher education departments. Often, the learning content of leisure courses is tackled in an informal way, which can increase everyone's enjoyment by encouraging participation.

Satisfaction is reward

There is satisfaction and pride to be derived from learning. Some of this satisfaction can be narrowed down to the fact that you gain in confidence through tackling something new, ambitious and demanding. Against all the odds – inexperience, lack of study skills, little time, no support, few funds – you make the effort and succeed, and can be justly proud of your achievement! Besides the satisfaction of knowing that you have achieved your aim, and that you have done it voluntarily, without coercion, you may also benefit from:

- being able to make appropriate use of your new knowledge

- understanding and using new technology

- having a wider, better-informed view on a subject and a broader base against which to assess new information

- improving your skills in interpreting information

- widening your vocational horizons and career prospects

- having renewed faith in your own abilities.

Some learning can give tangible benefits – think of re-creating excellent pastries in your own kitchen, the joy of playing an instrument or being able to upholster a favourite chair, or of impressing the boss by employing the most appropriate spreadsheets and graphs to display market research findings. Of course, as you acquire new skills, you may gain qualifications, certificates to display – even prizes! But, whether or not your learning is validated with certificates, the life-enhancing benefits of having succeeded through your own efforts will emerge with time!

> *'Coming back to learning has opened doors to other possibilities and opportunities – financially, intellectually and socially – that were closed to me in the past.'*

Academic improvement

Many people turn their thoughts to catching up on their general educational and basic skills levels only when they:

- need to find a job

- are planning to make a lifestyle change

- want to improve their prospects in work

- feel ready to make a career change.

Suddenly, it appears that 90% of job advertisements ask for computing skills, an ability with figures, good communication skills (maybe another language) and/or experience in customer service work – many potential employers seek people who can deal in a confident manner with clients and customers. It may be timely to look again at your levels of academic achievement, and to consider whether you might usefully upgrade your qualifications.

Basic skills

It is widely acknowledged that many people reach the end of their formal education still feeling unconfident about their reading and writing skills and their work with numbers. Low performance levels in basic skills may emerge only when people try to complete application forms in writing, search for jobs online or write speculative letters enquiring about work. Numerous people, from every kind of background, feel a need to improve their reading and comprehension skills, their grammar and spelling or, simply, their verbal and presentation skills. Many people who derived little benefit from their years in school decide, at a later date, to tackle and improve their low level of achievement in these basic skills. Some returners to learning want to be able to help their children achieve more from their schooling than they did themselves, and a feeling of ineffectiveness can challenge a parent's morale and provide the stimulus for self-improvement. Often, a renewed drive to learn arises from a need to find work. Usually, only a small amount of dedicated time with an encouraging teacher is needed for people to overcome obstacles to learning, once they actively want to learn. Any earlier problems that may have presented difficulties – such as an unhappy or stressful learning environment – will have been largely overcome in adulthood. Individual cases – where a learner may need specialist help – can be identified, and different approaches tried to provide appropriate assistance.

General education

Many employers request 'a good general education' from job applicants, not necessarily specifying any particular subjects or grades. But, depending on the number and quality of applications for a vacancy, employers may prefer, nevertheless, to recruit from amongst those who have achieved a grade C or above in GCSE mathematics, English, and, possibly, science or a practically-based subject. IT skills also are usually a bonus as almost every job currently advertised involves the use of computers – if only at a basic level.

Many adults return to learning to gain academic qualifications to satisfy entry requirements to careers or training, or for entry to further or higher education courses. Also, the impetus can come from a desire to make progress in work, where further qualifications are often necessary to achieve a higher-grade position, or, to make a career change.

With a complete range of qualifications, accrediting every stage of academic progress, it is possible to amass quite an array of certificates! The level of qualifications sought for entry to many careers has risen over time. Today, few jobs are advertised for which employers seek low-level or no formal qualifications. Many recruiters want highly-skilled, motivated self-starters – flexible workers who work well either on their own initiative or in a team.

A degree more

An increasing number of careers actually demand degree-level qualifications, and adults lacking the formal qualifications for degree course entry are now encouraged to enter the academic field through preparative or access courses that introduce ways to study and learn. Some professions require a specialised postgraduate qualification, before you can aspire to full professional status. If you have not previously felt motivated to raise your qualification levels, you might reconsider your position for the chance of an improvement in your financial prospects. There is plenty of accumulated evidence that there is a very worthwhile graduate premium, i.e. degree holders who are in graduate jobs – jobs which demand high levels of critical thinking and appraisal, information handling, analysis, self-motivation etc – are paid considerably higher salaries than their peers who only have level 3 (A level or equivalent) qualifications. A big majority of graduates surveyed recently said that a degree was still a good investment, despite student debts. Details of student funding in chapter five will help you to come to your own conclusions.

Rarified learning

Of course, some people simply love to learn! With this self-improving approach to study, the acquisition of knowledge becomes all-important, whether at GCSE level or through postgraduate academic research. This kind of learning we often talk of as 'learning for learning's sake' – the purpose of which can be to gain an informed view or opinion, or to encourage philosophical reflection – really, to become wiser.

Jessica Sewell – a passion for knowledge

Jessica is currently serving a prison sentence, but is using her time very productively to study a range of courses, which have benefited her personally as well as improving her job prospects upon release.

'My experiences on embarking on a return to learning have been prompted by some challenging obstacles, and my previously unfulfilling existence has been transformed. I have a new-found freedom, and my confidence has increased

---

tremendously. This is also helping me to gain a vision of what my new life might be like, so that I can be of benefit to society.

Throughout my twenties, I sought to return to learning, but was prevented from doing so by the invisible obstacles that invariably found themselves in my path, whether it be a matter of funding or a fear of being unable to succeed in the classroom. I also suffered a lack of encouragement. I am currently an inmate in Her Majesty's Prison Holloway, and even though every door had been previously shut, seemingly impenetrable doors to learning have been opened!

I have successfully re-entered the classroom and I am working towards A levels in both English and maths, with excellent tutors and instructors, I might add.

As a beginner, with a ten-year gap after leaving school, I must say excitedly that my experience of learning, within what many may regard as a less than desirable environment, has been most satisfactory! Overcoming faults, most of which were invariably resting upon my shoulders, has been a difficult journey. However, we must all endeavour to develop our aptitude for learning and personal growth. I am currently diligently studying a correspondence course in New Testament studies with the William Booth College, and working towards a Diploma in Religious Studies in association with the Salvation Army. I have also endeavoured to study successfully with The Open University and have been granted approval and met all the criteria for two courses in humanities towards the Diploma. This in-depth insight has given me an increased passion for knowledge, and greatly contributed to my own personal growth. I now have a goal in mind, and I am determined to complete my studies.

Returning to study has been an absolute joy, and has really improved my feelings of self-worth. Studying has brought meaning and a greater purpose to my life which will benefit both myself and, hopefully, others in the future. I consider it an honour and privilege to be able to return to study, and I plan to continue in this path which I have now started.'

Vocational learning

With the present emphasis on people raising their skill levels, there has been a push from the Government to encourage everybody to take their learning to as high a level as possible. The concept of lifelong learning has taken hold across the work culture.

Certainly, there have never been so many opportunities to gain skills and qualifications in the workplace. Many adults who fight shy of entering formal educational institutions find that they can happily accumulate evidence for accreditation of their skills in performing tasks in the workplace – and so gain nationally-recognised vocational qualifications. Credits can be awarded for prior acquisition of knowledge and skills in earlier employment or learning.

Adults under the age of 25 can join the Apprenticeships and Advanced Apprenticeships designed for young people, and there are also Apprenticeships for Adults being trialled from September 2004. Through this route, you can match the level of qualification gained by learners following full-time vocational courses in further education colleges (all of which are, of course, open to adults). Older adults can also embark on Work-based Learning for Adults programmes. This type of training has the advantage of providing useful work experience, plus an income!

Further education courses, combined with the range of distance- or open-learning options made available through multimedia, create a vast array of vocational learning opportunities! If you are interested in taking a course to ease your entry to employment, then almost anything is possible. You will have to pick your way carefully through directories, databases and prospectuses, and may well need guidance in interpreting which courses are most appropriate for increasing your employability.

If you are in employment, you may be offered the opportunity to further your occupational skills through in-house training, being sent on training courses by your employer, or through broadening your abilities with distance-learning courses. Larger or expanding companies are more likely to have a proactive policy regarding employee training and lifelong learning, being keen to encourage a highly-skilled and motivated workforce.

Vocational courses all have a large practical element and can help you to:

- prepare for entry to the world of work

- build up your key skills

- update your skills, or re-skill, to gain the capabilities that employers seek today

- prepare for voluntary work

- build subject interests into occupational strengths

- improve your job skills and level of working

- help you acquire the business skills essential for self employment

- work towards a supervisory/management-level qualification

- train to a highly-skilled level in a specific craft

- accumulate credits for your skills in using IT as a tool.

Other benefits of learning

Don't feel that all your learning has to enhance your employability. Although position and salary are important, they are not everything in life. There is life beyond work!

If all the previous reasons for returning to learning are not enough for you, perhaps the fact that learning has been shown to improve health and well-being may convince you. There's even a Government-funded body, the Centre for Research on the Wider Benefits of Learning, looking into the benefits to learners' health and parenting skills, among other things. So, what's stopping you?

> '…and my advice to anyone thinking of returning to learning – just do it.'

Further information

Planning a Career Change – published by How to Books, £9.99.

Study Skills for Adult Learners – published by How to Books, £10.99.

Chapter two
Ways to learn

Chapter one looked at the reasons why people return to learning; in this chapter, the emphasis is on the different ways of studying. In recent years, the opportunities for adults wanting to return to learning have increased greatly. This is due in part to a much more flexible approach by colleges, universities and other learning providers.

- There is greater scope to study for all types of qualifications on a part-time basis or through open learning.

- It is easier to transfer between courses.

- It is becoming more common to get accepted to courses on the basis of a much wider range of previous learning and work experience than just academic qualifications.

There is a wide choice of what you can study, how you study and where you can study.

When you are trying to decide on the right course for you, a practical consideration will be the way the course is **organised** and **delivered**. This will have a large bearing on whether it can be successfully combined with your current work and/or domestic responsibilities. Make sure you find a course that suits your **personal circumstances**. A successful outcome to your learning can depend as much on finding the course that suits your personal circumstances as it does on finding a course offering the right subjects at the right level for you.

Courses are available in the following ways: full-time, part-time, (day and/or evening), short courses, and through distance and open learning. In recent years, learning providers have increasingly recognised that choice and flexibility is important for adults. The best institutions make efforts to structure courses accordingly. For instance, they may run programmes at evenings and weekends or on a part-time basis, or schedule classes so parents can take and collect children to and from school.

The rest of the chapter looks at the main 'ways' to learn.

Full-time study

Returning to full-time learning requires making sacrifices but, as many mature students find, it can be enormously satisfying – read the accounts of their experiences written by Emma and Wayne on pages 71 and 14. There are definite advantages, not least that by making the commitment to a full-time course you may be more able to make the most of education, benefiting from regular contact and support from tutors and fellow students and using educational facilities to the full. Additionally, full-time study usually offers the quickest route to qualifications.

It can be tough financially. You may have to pay the full cost of the course; you may be asked to contribute towards tuition fees. You will need to be able to support yourself while learning. You may be eligible for a student loan to help towards your living costs, or be eligible for some other forms of financial support through the college/university, which could help. See chapter five for more information about financial support while learning.

Full-time does not necessarily mean nine-to-five attendance, five days a week. In higher education (post A level and equivalent), most courses at colleges and universities involve substantial amounts of independent study and learning; lectures, seminars, tutorials etc may account for as little as half the week. The academic year only occupies between 30 and 33 weeks of the year, so there is time to attend to the rest of your life. Indeed, many students manage to combine part-time or shift work with a full-time course, although this is usually through economic necessity rather than choice. It can be difficult for mature students with family responsibilities to fit paid work alongside course and family commitments.

Your family may have to make sacrifices as well – certainly, you will need to find time to study – so it is very important at the outset to get their backing and support. For strategies on coping successfully have a look at chapter seven.

Rhonda Reid – flying high with media

Rhonda is studying an access to media course with a view to progressing to a degree course in media studies.

'I am aged 36 and currently on an access to media course. Sometimes I wish I hadn't been such a rebel at school, as I would have been able to go straight to university. Sometimes I feel as if I am back at school. There is a 13-year age gap between myself the oldest and the second oldest – most of the other students are much younger.

I decided to go back to learning when I realised that my CV had far too many gaps, and I didn't want to spend the rest of my life working in an office as a secretary, which I had never really enjoyed. I was also getting tired of getting nowhere in pursuit of my ambitions as a performer and also tired doing the 'knowledge' with A-Z in hand every other week looking for some record company offices, audition venue alongside the routine of doing office work, which I did not enjoy.

Anyway I discovered I had another 'talent' – for ideas and writing. I am enthusiastic about my future prospects when I receive my BA Hons in creative writing/journalism and news media in three years' time. I have had an article published in the local paper and in the college staff newsletter since starting this course. I am also excited, as I have been accepted into a good university, which is recognised for creative writing. There is also the opportunity to learn French and to study abroad. I am not, however, looking forward to how I will finance myself as a student, living on a student loan.

Returning to study may mean a lack of money, as it can be difficult to find an employer who can offer you work which fits around college hours. Your social life can also suffer, as you are always consumed with course work. But I say "Go for it." Life begins at 40. By that time I want to be working on a soap/drama, submitting articles to magazines and eventually writing a best selling novel.'

Studying part-time

The obvious advantage of part-time study is that it is easier to combine study with work and domestic responsibilities. You have the opportunity to study for much the same range of qualifications without making the rather greater commitment demanded by full-time learning. The downside is that it usually takes longer to obtain qualifications. Many qualifications, in particular those offered by professional bodies, are only available through part-time courses.

The term 'part-time' covers a multitude of arrangements. These include:

- **part-time half-day** (e.g. attending one morning or afternoon a week) – vocational courses and some leisure courses (i.e. courses undertaken for interest) are available on this basis, as are some A level/GCSE courses (perhaps involving joining full-time students in their classes)

- **part-time full-day** – includes **day-release** courses, aimed at those in employment who are supported by their employers to gain relevant vocational qualifications

- **shortened day** (e.g. classes that fit between school hours) – return to learn courses and part-time access to higher education courses (see chapter three) are examples of courses that may be available on this basis

- **day/evening combined** – perhaps one afternoon and one evening a week – often vocational courses are offered on this basis an alternative to day-release, so students are only away from their workplace (assuming they work '9-5') for half a day a week

- **evening** classes (where you attend generally one evening a week for two/three hours) – vocational subjects, GCSEs, AS and A levels as well as leisure and recreation courses are all available on this basis

- **block-release** – aimed at those in employment, who attend college e.g. one- or two-week 'blocks' several times a year to gain vocational qualifications.

The above are all 'taught' courses i.e. the traditional situation, learning alongside a group of others following the same course, led by a teacher/

tutor/lecturer. But part-time learning can also be undertaken through more flexible and independent forms of learning – such as through distance and open learning, described later in this chapter.

The extent to which the above options are available to you depends on the subject/qualification you are aiming at, and what the institutions local to you offer. If considering GCSE and A level courses, you may well have the choice between part-time during the day, or part-time evening courses (as well as the choice of open or distance learning routes). Many part-time higher education courses will require some attendance during the day, although some courses are offered on an evening-only basis. For example, it is possible to gain a degree through part-time evening study in subjects such as English, history, management, computing and even (at Birkbeck, University of London) in scientific subjects!

Modular courses

Many courses, whether full-time, part-time or distance learning, are organised on a modular basis i.e. they are sub-divided up into many parts, often called units or modules. Each of the units or modules covers a particular aspect of a course. This structure allows you to build up unit by unit towards a qualification, and can provide many more options about what, how and when you study – for example, you can build up your modules at a pace to suit yourself. This type of learning is especially attractive to people with other commitments.

In higher education, many courses are offered on a modular basis. Certain modules may be compulsory – or you may have a free choice of which modules to take. Each module has a specific credit rating. Students build up 'credit' towards a degree by successfully completing individual modules. In higher education, Credit Accumulation and Transfer Schemes (known as CATS) allow the retention and transfer of credit for the modules that have already been passed. This means, if a student wishes or has to change courses, move to another institution or take a break from study, all is not lost – as they are given credit for the successful learning they have already undertaken.

More about Credit Accumulation and Transfer Schemes in chapter three.

Short courses

Short courses can be full-time or part-time. In some ways, short courses combine some of the advantages of full-time and part-time study.

- You can pack a great deal of learning into an intensive short course.

- You may find a spell of concentrated study on a two-week course preferable to studying on a day-release basis over 10 or more weeks.

- You can take courses as and when you need to learn.

- They do not require the commitment demanded by longer courses.

For these reasons, short courses have been favoured by many employers as a means of training staff. Private training companies, as well as colleges and universities, compete vigorously for the short-course market – providing courses for business and industry in areas such as marketing, computing, management training and languages. These range from one-day seminars and workshops through to one-week or two-week programmes run on a day attendance or residential basis.

Both colleges and private training organisations run short courses providing additional skills and knowledge to those who already have experience and skills in their chosen occupation – in areas from plumbing to hairdressing.

There are also short courses on offer to the individual learner – particularly in subjects undertaken for leisure and interest. Such courses run for anything from half a day, through weekend courses, to one-week courses, which may be residential.

Short part-time courses, particularly those aimed at returners to learning, are a very effective way of developing new skills and restoring confidence.

Distance, open and independent learning

Distance/open learning (or flexible learning as it may be called) is, in many ways, an attractive option in that it allows you to study in your own time and at your own pace. You can organise your learning around your other commitments, using prepared learning materials rather than attending traditional classes with a group of others. You can study at home, or perhaps through an open learning centre, if you need access to a computer. However, you generally also have the support and back-up from a tutor. Courses are available at all levels, from basic to postgraduate.

Typically, distance/open learning consists of working through learning materials (workbooks etc) and, perhaps, using video and audio cassettes; there are also many courses delivered through computer-based packages – via CD or online. Assignments may be sent to your tutor for assessment.

Given the advantages, it is perhaps no surprise that open learning is regarded as an increasingly important way to deliver learning. However, some people might find there are drawbacks.

- If you are not self-disciplined it is easy to drop courses as other pressures or interests arise.

- It can be isolating – if you are learning at home, you can miss the stimulus of fellow students.

- Depending on the tutor support arrangements available, you may find tutor contact is not as easily accessible or as immediate as on a traditional course.

This is why simple teach-yourself packages are rarely entirely effective. To be successful as a learning medium, flexible-learning packages need:

- good support and backup from tutors

- a unit or assignment structure to encourage learners to progress step by step

- opportunities to work with other students in workshops, tutorials or summer schools

- a range of different learning materials with practical exercises.

In practice, you have two broad options.

Distance learning

You can choose to study at home, enrolling on a course offered by a distance learning organisation. The best courses provide you with learning materials and self-study packs, tutorial support and a system for assessing and marking your assignments. Leaders in distance learning include the Open University, the National Extension College and the Open College of the Arts.

Distance education is clearly suitable for those who live a long way from the nearest college or university, or for those who want to study independently at home. The success of the Open University shows that this option has widespread appeal. There is more about the OU in chapter four.

Open learning

Open learning allows you to study at a time to suit yourself, independently, using specially-written materials, but with tutor support. You can learn through flexible learning packages, usually using a computer, at local open learning centres, or if you prefer, at home. At open learning centres, there will be tutors on hand to guide you through the materials and to help you with any problems. Centres may be based in colleges or in other venues within the community. You may have heard of learndirect courses, or learndirect centres. There are a range of learndirect courses, which you access via a computer, and can either follow by attending a learndirect centre, at a time to suit you, or you can undertake on your computer at home. More about learndirect in chapter four.

Craig Brown – opening doors through open learning

Craig, 30, is a salesperson looking for a change of career. When a colleague told him about learndirect, Craig jumped at the chance to gain more skills and work towards his goal of becoming a teacher. Craig has gone on to take careers advice which led to him starting on the

---

ladder of qualifications towards becoming a teacher. He plans to get some practical teaching experience to back this up.

'*I like learning but I missed a lot of school through illness. I've tried night classes, but they're so inflexible I soon gave up. learndirect is different, because you can make it fit round other commitments. I've always wanted to go into teaching, but I didn't think I'd have a chance because I don't have the right skills or the right qualifications. learndirect has given me both.*

Being given the chance to do a qualification in literacy is fantastic. My English has always been good, and now I have the paper to prove it. Doing the test online is a natural progression from doing the learndirect courses online. If that's how you've been studying it makes sense you do the test in the same way – it's familiar so there's less pressure. Giving someone a pen and paper can be really daunting because it brings back bad memories of school exams.

The centre has been fantastic, and getting my literacy qualification has been a great confidence booster. I'd recommend anyone to go to learndirect and have chat, they'll start you at the right level on the right course, and there really is something for everyone.

I meet a lot of people in my job, and being a people person is one of the reasons I want to go into teaching. Communication is key in the classroom, as is building confidence. You don't know what your potential is unless you're given the chance to achieve it. That's something I have first-hand experience of, and I want to pass it on to others.

Out of every hundred people I meet, 99 of them say they want to retrain. Only a very small percentage actually go and do something about it. My message to them is don't just say it – do it.'

Other independent learning

There are different ways to learn which you can do independently, without the benefit of any tutorial support – through books, CDs, videos, TV and computer packages. This is perhaps a more difficult route, as you do not have any specialist advice and support, but it is a good way to learn if travelling to a learning centre is a problem, or the time you can devote to learning is limited.

- There are plenty of teach-yourself books, computer handbooks etc on the market.

- Tapes and CDs are a good way of learning, particularly a language, as it's always beneficial to hear the language spoken. Look out for the costs involved – you may need to buy several tapes or CDs to complete a course.

- There are computer packages that cover a wide range of subjects. You can also learn computer skills this way.

- Another way to learn is in your own home, through the television and radio. BBC and Channel 4 transmit educational programmes – for instance, during the BBC's night-time 'Learning Zone'. Sometimes, books and videos are available to go with the programmes. There are also online resources provided by the BBC and Channel 4 – see www.bbc.co.uk/learningzone and www.channel4.com/learning for more information.

Employment-based courses

Employers often use courses based on company premises to train their staff – to update skills, learn new skills, to keep abreast of new developments, computer packages etc. These courses may be delivered by other employees, or 'bought' in from training providers. The length of these courses varies, but the vast majority are short and tailor made. Some employers have open learning centres based in their premises, where employees may follow learning packages (via a computer) at a pace to suit themselves.

Work-based Learning for Adults (Training for Work in Scotland) is a government-funded training programme for people aged 25 and over who have been unemployed for six months or more (although earlier entry is possible for some). Individual training plans are drawn up according to need. The plans may include job-specific training, work experience or basic employability training. Benefits plus an allowance are paid. Northern Ireland also has similar programmes. Find out more about Work-based Learning for Adults in chapter four.

And finally....

When considering ways to learn, think about:

- whether full-time learning is an option open to you, and would suit you – or would some form of part-time learning suit you better?

- would you prefer the flexibility of an open- or distance-learning approach – or do you feel that the more traditional style of attending classes with other students is the way for you?

Remember to research all the options, and go for the one that best fits in with your lifestyle, commitments and favoured approach to learning.

Chapter three
The qualification maze

When looking at prospectuses, course directories and databases, the number of different qualifications on offer can be confusing. And, to make matters worse, they are usually known by their initials!

This chapter answers the following questions.

- How do these different qualifications relate to each other?

- How can you be sure whether a particular qualification is recognised?

- How can you be certain which is the right qualification for **you**?

Happily, there has been a considerable effort in recent years to introduce more coherence in the qualification system. There is a national framework of qualifications in place for England, Wales, and Northern Ireland. A new National Qualifications Framework (NQF) came into effect in September 2004. Scotland already has its new framework in place. These frameworks should make it easier to see how any particular qualification you are considering relates to other qualifications, and plot possible progression routes from one qualification level to the next.

Getting to grips with the basics...

Qualifications range from the **academic,** such as history or English, through to the highly **vocational.** Some vocational courses are fairly broad based e.g. business studies or health and social care, whilst others are specific to a particular occupation e.g. plumbing or accountancy. GCSEs and A levels are examples of academic qualifications; while they do not qualify you for a

particular job, they indicate a general level of academic achievement. Qualifications such as NVQs (National Vocational Qualifications), however, relate to a particular occupation. Qualifications are also divided into a number of different levels, from basic-skill level through to professional-level.

Which qualification?

A checklist of questions

- Do you want to aim at a general academic qualification, or something work-related?

- If aiming at work-related qualifications, do you want a broad-based qualification, or a qualification related to a specific occupational area?

- What level of qualification are you aiming for?

- Do you have the necessary entry requirements (where applicable) or suitable experience to allow you to enter a course at that level?

- Will any of your previous qualifications or experience give you any exemptions from parts of the course?

- Is the qualification recognised by employers and relevant professional bodies?

- Do you need to 'brush up' on any aspects e.g. study skills or maths, prior to starting the course?

This chapter outlines the range of qualifications available across the UK. Qualifications available in England, Wales and Northern Ireland are described initially, followed by a word about accreditation of prior learning, credit transfer schemes and open college networks. The Scottish qualification system is described at the end.

It is, of course, only possible within this book to give a broad outline of the main qualifications available. You can follow up the information provided here by consulting some of the references listed at the end of the chapter, and by talking to course providers and contacting the relevant examining body.

The Credit and Qualifications Framework for Wales (CQFW) was launched in 2003, and all accredited learning will gradually be brought into it. The CQFW sees Wales introducing new qualifications, such as the Welsh Baccalaureate (known as the Welsh Bac). It ties in with the NQF. For more information see www.elwa.ac.uk for information about the framework and www.wbq.org.uk for more about the Welsh Bac.

Qualifications in England, Wales and Northern Ireland

To set the scene...

The list below is a simplified version of the NQF that took effect from September 2004. It gives you a general idea of the equivalencies. As you will see, qualifications are banded into different levels.

Entry level: Certificates of educational achievement; basic skills

Level 1: GCSEs at grades D-G; NVQ level 1; basic skills

Level 2: GCSEs at grades A*-C; NVQ level 2

Level 3: A levels; NVQ level 3

Levels 4 – 8: higher education qualifications, including Higher National Diplomas/Certificates, Diplomas of Higher Education, foundation degrees, degrees and postgraduate qualifications; professional qualifications; NVQ levels 4 and 5.

Vocational certificates and diplomas, and key skills are available at all levels throughout the framework.

Basic skills and key skills qualifications

Many opportunities are provided for those who need to brush up on their basic literacy and numeracy skills. Courses are often run by adult and community education providers, and through further education colleges. The following are some examples of the available qualifications in basic skills such as literacy and numeracy, and qualifications that relate to the important six key skills of communication, application of number, IT, working with others, problem solving and improving own learning and performance.

- **City and Guilds certificates** – these include the Wordpower and Numberpower Certificates. Each is available at four levels.

- **Key Skills qualifications** – you can start at a basic level, but then can work your way up, as each of the six key skills can be certified at each of the levels of the NQF.

- **OCR National Skills Profile** – certificates key skills and personal and practical work skills at entry level, related to a number of vocational areas.

While being a qualification in its own right, a key skills qualification will usually be taken alongside qualifications such as AS and A levels, Apprenticeships and NVQs.

Janice Lawrence – taking her first step forward

Janice decided on a Return to Learn course to improve her general standard of education, build her confidence and prepare her for a return to the workplace.

The need to return to employment after years of full-time parenting was creeping ever closer, and the prospects of achieving this was quite daunting. The opportunity to learn new skills and improve my standard of education was what I was looking for, and to achieve this, I would have to gain qualifications. I decided to take the plunge and return to learning to allow me to fulfil this goal.

Being out of the education system for so long was a worrying aspect for me. Having lost confidence and being computer-illiterate was not helping the situation. I decided to enrol on a short course. 'Return to Learn' looked to be the ideal course for me. A 10-week course, one session a week, which gave the option of improving basic skills in English and/or computing, was just what I was looking for.

Being honest, I put off this moment on numerous occasions. This probably sounds ridiculous, but it took a lot of courage to take this first step and even a few sleepless nights. Having taken the plunge, I haven't looked back. The support and encouragement given on this course helped to build my confidence. Having completed this course, I went on to 'Back to Work' and passed CLAIT 1 in IT. I have just finished 'Effective Business Writing' and have enrolled on the 'Microsoft Office for Improvers'.

The benefits for me personally have been enormous, and in the future I feel I will benefit both in job satisfaction and financially. My advice to anyone contemplating enrolling on a course is to find out as much as possible about the course before you commit yourself. Consider the amount of homework required, any cost you might incur, or most importantly, is this course for you? Time taken at this stage will help to eliminate the possibility of a bad experience! Don't take on anything you feel you're going to struggle with, set yourself goals, be positive and you will enjoy the experience.

If time is on your side, invest it wisely and enrol on one of the short part-time courses available, some of which are free. This way, you're not committed to anything long term and the rewards are instant, giving you a sense of achievement and, in some cases, credit in the form of a recognised certificate.'

National Vocational Qualifications (NVQs)

National Vocational Qualifications (NVQs) are occupational qualifications, which have been introduced over recent years and now cover almost every area of employment. NVQs are competence based, meaning that each qualification is assessed on whether you can meet agreed standards in specified skills, tasks or areas of work. Here, compared with academic courses, it may be easier to get credit for previously acquired learning. You gain NVQs by simply demonstrating that you are competent in particular skill areas to the required standard.

The situation is comparable to learning to drive: the test is not concerned with how long it takes to learn, nor where or how you are taught, but simply on whether you can demonstrate that you can drive to a given standard. It is, therefore, possible to gain an NVQ through assessment in your workplace, without attending a course or sitting any exams. The NVQ approach has a number of attractive features for adults. It makes it easier to recognise past achievement: you get credit for those skills that you have already acquired both through work and through periods of education and training. It allows you to work towards qualifications over time: each NVQ comprises several units, for which you claim and carry forward credit as you achieve the required standards. It allows you some choice over how you learn: you can work towards qualifications through a combination of work experience, on-the-job training, private study and attendance at college. For details of NVQs:

- consult the QCA (Qualifications and Curriculum Agency) website: www.qca.org.uk or their qualifications database: www.openquals.org.uk

- your local Learning and Skills Council, or Sector Skills Council can also provide information.

GCSEs

GCSE (General Certificate of Secondary Education) exams are, of course, the academic qualifications taken by young people in their last year of compulsory schooling. They indicate a general level of achievement in a range of academic subjects e.g. English, science, French.

As an adult, you can study for a wide range of GCSEs in evening classes run by colleges and adult education centres, or through open and distance learning. A huge range of subjects are on offer, including subjects like psychology, health studies and sociology. You don't need to have studied the subject before. The standard syllabus for students at school lasts two years, but courses available through adult education programmes generally aim for the syllabus to be covered in one year.

Assessment is through a combination of coursework and exams. GCSEs are graded from A* to G; often grades C or above will be sought for entry to higher-level courses (although these requirements may be relaxed for adults). If you are returning to learning, and are looking for a general academic course, GCSEs can be a good starting point.

GCSEs in vocational subjects first appeared in 2002, with the first awards being made in the summer of 2004. Designed to replace GNVQs, these GCSEs are more practical, and largely coursework-based. They are available in eight areas including engineering, manufacturing and applied art and design. They are double award GCSEs.

'My English has always been good, and now I have the paper to prove it' says one returner.

AS and A levels

GCE A (Advanced) levels are well-known nationally-recognised academic awards which provide entry to a range of jobs and to higher education courses (e.g. university degrees – although, again, the message for adult readers is that A level entry requirements are often relaxed for mature applicants).

With regard to structure, each A level consists of six separate units (in effect, mini-courses). Each unit is separately assessed. The first half of an A level course is made up of three AS (Advanced Subsidiary) units, and successful completion of these leads to an AS level qualification. The second half of the A level course comprises three further units, called A2 units, to complete the A level course.

AS and A levels are available in a similar range of subjects to GCSEs. There are a few subjects (e.g. critical thinking) available at AS level only. Some subjects at AS/A level, such as maths, physics and French, build on the knowledge gained at GCSE (or through equivalent courses). However, there are a number of subjects that you can take at A level which do not require previous knowledge of the subject, such as law, psychology and sociology.

Adults may take AS and A levels through part-time day or evening classes offered by further education colleges and adult education services, or through open or distance learning. AS levels usually take a year to complete, and the full A level takes two years, although some more intensive courses may be available. Assessment is through coursework and exams. While many adults take A levels, adults aiming at entry to higher education may find a specially designed Access course more appropriate.

From September 2005, what were previously known as vocational A levels are being restructured to match A/S and A levels. They will no longer be known as vocational A levels, simply A levels. Subjects like applied science, travel and tourism, applied business and engineering provide an introduction to a broad vocational area.

Advanced extension awards (AEAs) are for those who are likely to get an A grade at A level and from 2006 will count towards UCAS points (more information on UCAS is contained in chapter seven).

The Access route

Access courses prepare adults who do not have the necessary qualifications for entry to higher education courses, such as degrees. They provide an alternative to taking A levels, and are specially designed for adults who may not have done any studying for some time, so build in plenty of assistance with developing study skills. Typically, Access courses last one year full-time, and two years part-time. They are usually run through further education colleges, although some are provided by higher education institutions, and adult residential colleges run similar preparatory courses. Some Access courses prepare students for entry to a broad range of arts and humanities courses, others to science courses. There are also many specific Access courses – geared to entry in a particular subject area, e.g. nursing, social sciences, teaching. Courses often have established links with particular higher education courses. It is a good idea to check that Access courses of interest to you are 'kitemarked' i.e. approved by the Quality Assurance Agency for Higher Education.

Gary Smyth – caring for his future

Gary is studying an access to nursing course, having already been accepted onto a degree course in Nursing.

'It had been over twenty years since I experienced any kind of formal education, having left school after sitting A Levels. I had intended to pursue a career in the caring field, but because of various commitments and distractions I took a variety of jobs, including running my own business, all of which were interesting but not completely fulfilling. When I gained a job as a carer for the elderly and mentally infirm, my interest in mental health nursing was rekindled. By then I thought I

was too old being nearly forty, but was reassured and encouraged to become a nurse, so I managed to enrol on a university Access course.

Since returning to education I am delighted to be learning among other mature students. This course has enabled me to meet new people with similar interest and goals. Although it can be difficult finding time to study whilst holding down a full-time job, I have found learning to be a joyful experience. This has greatly surprised me, as I had felt disenchanted with education when I left school. Now I look forward to going and can appreciate the expertise of my tutors, who in their methods and efforts convey a great willingness for us to succeed while encouraging a friendly and relaxed environment.

The experience of learning has been a delight, even sitting exams! I have been able to test myself and I am overjoyed to have done so well, having already been accepted to study a degree in nursing at a university.

If you have an inclination to return to learning, whether it be to pursue a career or for the experience of learning something new and of interest, I can heartily recommend that you go and do it. If you are a mature student like me, you will experience the joy of learning new things and the comradeship of a group of people helping and supporting one another; but bring a packed lunch! School dinners have yet to evolve.'

GNVQs (General National Vocational Qualifications)

GNVQs are being withdrawn in three stages from 2005 – 2007.

BTEC qualifications

BTEC qualifications, awarded by Edexcel, are work-related qualifications. They cover a huge range of vocational areas, some are fairly broad e.g. business, building studies; others are very specific e.g. interior design, printing. BTEC qualifications are awarded as Awards, Diplomas or Certificates – which can be studied either full- or part- time.

- **BTEC Introductory** qualifications are the equivalent of GCSE D to G grade, at level 1 of the National Qualifications Framework.

- **BTEC First** qualifications are at GCSE A* to C level, at level 2.

- **BTEC National** qualifications are equivalent to A levels, or level 3 standard, and can provide entry to higher education or employment. BTEC Nationals can be given as Awards, as well as Certificates and Diplomas of 6, 12 and 18 units respectively. They are included in the UCAS points tariff for entry to HE.

- **BTEC Higher National** qualifications are at higher education level. They aim to prepare students for work at technician, supervisory and management level. A year of further study can lead to a degree. There are no set entry requirements, but admissions tutors usually look for one A level, NVQ level 3, BTEC National or equivalent. Entry qualifications are generally relaxed for mature applicants with relevant experience.

- **BTEC Diploma** qualifications such as BTEC Diploma in Management Studies are also available, and are usually taken by professionals wishing to improve their skills in a subject.

Along with other exam bodies, BTEC (through Edexcel) awards foundation degrees in various subjects. See the section on foundation degrees later in this chapter for more details.

Other vocational qualifications

There is a range of other work-related qualifications besides those already mentioned. The value of any professional or vocational qualification depends upon its reputation with employers or within a profession. Always be cautious of any diplomas that are awarded by the college itself, rather than by a national body, and check out their acceptability with potential employers. Some well-regarded vocational qualifications include those awarded by:

- **OCR** (Oxford, Cambridge and RSA Examinations): besides awarding a wide range of academic and vocational qualifications (including NVQs), OCR offers the well-known RSA qualifications of office and business skills.

- **City and Guilds**: provide a wide range of qualifications, related to business and industry (including NVQs). The City and Guilds group includes **Pitman Qualifications** (business and commerce) and **Institute of Leadership and Management (ILM)** (management and development qualifications).

- **London Chamber of Commerce and Industry Examinations Board:** LCCI qualifications are offered in all aspects of business, including secretarial and administrative, accounting and management.

Diplomas of Higher Education (DipHE)

These are higher education qualifications requiring two years' full-time study. Students who successfully complete a DipHE may take a further year of study to top up to a degree. There are far fewer DipHE courses than degree courses. It is possible to take a DipHE in academic subjects, such as history and English; often courses leading to DipHE are covering more than one subject e.g DipHE in geography and tourism, psychology and health, in combined studies, for example. Some professional courses in vocational areas like nursing, youth work and operating department practice also lead to a DipHE award. Entry requirements are as for a degree.

Certificates in Higher Education may be awarded after the equivalent of one year of study at higher education level.

Degrees

A degree is the standard entry requirement for many professional and managerial careers. The award of a degree has wide currency and opens many doors. The range of subjects available is immense, ranging from the highly academic, such as classical studies, through to the highly vocational, such as town and country planning. Some are very broad-based, e.g. combined studies, while others are very specialised e.g. animation. Degrees require at least three years' study, longer if you study on a part-time basis. Some are offered as sandwich courses, with study interspersed with spells in industry and commerce. Many degrees are structured on a modular basis, allowing you to choose what topics to study, specialising as you go along.

Higher education establishments welcome mature students (usually defined as entrants aged 21 or over) and entry requirements may be relaxed. (The stated minimum requirements for entry by young people are two A levels or equivalent, plus supporting GCSEs.) As a mature applicant, admissions tutors will want to satisfy themselves that you have the ability to cope with the demands of the course. They will therefore look at what you have achieved in the past, and some evidence of recent study is also important. Many adult students prepare themselves by following a specially designed Access course (mentioned previously in this chapter).

> *'I wasn't sure if it was feasible to plunge straight into a subject that sounded as grand and complex as 'astrophysics', it seemed way out of my league!'*

Foundation degrees

Foundation degrees are awarded in around 1100 vocational subjects, designed particularly to meet the skill requirements of industry and commerce. Foundation degrees are delivered flexibly, to meet the needs of people who wish to combine study with employment. They are therefore available through full- and part-time study and through distance learning. Studying full-time, they take two years to complete. There are no nationally set entry requirements for entry to a foundation degree course though individual courses may set their own requirements.

Although foundation degrees are a qualification in their own right, it is possible to achieve an honours degree through twelve or 15 months further study. The Government intends to make foundation degrees 'the main work-focused higher education qualification'.

The UCAS website contains lots of information on foundation degrees www.ucas.ac.uk as does the Foundation Degree Forward website: www.fdf.ac.uk

Postgraduate awards

Postgraduate courses divide into three broad categories: Master's degrees and doctorates, which are both higher degrees, and postgraduate diplomas or certificates.

The number of **Master's degree courses** has mushroomed in recent years. For example, MBA (Master of Business Administration) programmes are now commonplace. Many master's degrees are 'taught masters', requiring, typically, a year's full-time study including a dissertation or extended work-based project. Many are designed for people with some work and professional experience rather than new graduates. Other Master's degrees are awarded following a research project.

Postgraduate diplomas and certificates are usually vocational awards. Some may be required for entry to particular professions, e.g. the PGCE for entry to teaching.

Doctorate degrees (e.g. PhDs) are awarded after doing several years' research in a particular subject.

Professional bodies

Many professional bodies set their own examinations and qualifications. Achieving their qualifications leads to membership of that particular professional body, and is often obligatory if you want to enter a particular career, or to progress to a further level within a particular field of work. For example, to work in town planning, you need to complete a course accredited by the Royal Town Planning Institute. Professional qualifications are gradually being brought into the NVQ structure, although most remain outside it. This does not make them any less valuable, it simply reflects that they are not organised in a way that meets NVQ criteria.

Accreditation of prior learning

You may get credit towards (or exemption from) part of courses, for previous study or less formal learning that you have undertaken. Unlike the waiving of standard entry requirements, this necessarily requires a more involved process. In colleges and universities, this process is known by one of two acronyms, APL – the Accreditation of Prior Learning or APEL – the Accreditation of Prior Experiential Learning. APL and APEL can therefore give you recognition or 'credit' for the skills and knowledge that you have already gained.

Typically, you will be required to complete a portfolio with supporting documentation to demonstrate that you have acquired the relevant knowledge and learning. You might also be required to undergo a number of assessments. It may not always be worth going through this process, as it can be lengthy and it may be expensive.

However, it is always worth asking whether any relevant previous study and experience you may have can be formerly recognised (as the arrangements may vary from institution to institution). It could save repeating areas of study you have already covered.

Credit Accumulation and Transfer Schemes

CATS, as they are known, operate in many universities and higher education colleges. Courses are increasingly 'modularised' i.e. broken down into separate modules or minicourses, as described in chapter two. Each module is worth a number of credit points, usually rated at a particular level. You build up your total of credit points by completing individual modules, until you gain sufficient credit points at the correct levels to be awarded a particular qualification.

This system allows you the flexibility to change courses, for example, without necessarily losing 'credit' for what you have achieved so far. It can also allow you to swap between full- and part-time study. If you wish, or need, to move to another institution or take a break from study, the CATS system allows you to retain and transfer credit for the modules that you have already passed. CATS also offers more opportunities within a course; your degree course may require you to take certain core subjects but you may be able to take a much wider range of optional modules providing you accumulate sufficient credit points for the degree. Previous study that you have undertaken may also be assessed and given credit points.

At higher education level, Scotland has one scheme (SCOTCAT), which involves all Scottish universities and higher education institutes; while there are a variety of schemes operating in the rest of the UK. Enquire about such schemes at any colleges or universities to which you are thinking of applying.

Open College Networks (OCNs)

Open College Networks accredit qualifications offered through colleges and other learning providers in their particular geographical area. There are 28 local Networks in operation across England, Wales and Northern Ireland.

OCNs accredit courses from basic level through to Access courses. They offer you a way to get credit for learning that you may have done on a formal course, in the workplace, through a training programme or via voluntary work. The National Open College Network operates a framework of four levels of achievement. Each credit awarded represents 30 hours of learning, and is accredited at one of four levels. You can build up credits as you study, at a level appropriate to you. Such accreditation systems allow accreditation of learning that may not be formerly certificated elsewhere, and make it easier to progress from one learning opportunity to another. It makes for much easier comparison between courses. www.nocn.org.uk has more information.

Scottish qualifications

Scottish qualifications are organised into 12 levels within the Scottish Credit and Qualifications framework. Level one is designed to include those with severe and profound learning difficulties, and level twelve indicates doctoral studies. The levels are not related to years of study spent on gaining a qualification.

The idea is that subjects are available at each of the levels, and students can move up to the next level of difficulty on successful completion of their current level. The system can allow for people to study at different levels in different subjects. The framework has a detailed website which gives more information: www.scqf.org.uk. Further information on Scottish qualifications can also be found on the learndirect website: www.learndirectscotland.com.

Brief descriptions of the main qualifications are listed below.

Standard Grades

This is the equivalent qualification to GCSE, offered in a similar range of subjects. Adults may take Standard Grades through further education colleges. Assessment is normally through a mixture of formal examination and assessed coursework. Standard Grades are awarded from level 1 to level 7, where level 1 is the highest. Grade 3 roughly equates to a C at GCSE.

National Qualifications at Higher level

Scottish Higher Grades have traditionally been taken after one year of further study following Standard Grades, and provide entry to Scottish universities. Full-time students usually take five Highers, which are available in a wide range of academic and vocational subjects.

National Qualifications at Advanced Higher level

This qualification replaced the Certificate of Sixth Year Studies in 2002. While following on from Highers, the Advanced Higher is a free-standing qualification, so you do not need to have completed the Higher course before starting the Advanced Higher.

National Units, Courses and Group Awards

- **National Units** are available over a wide range of vocational fields. Most Units are 40 hours long; although some are 20, and others possibly 80. They are completed by assessments marked by teachers and lecturers on a pass or fail basis.

- **National Courses** are made up of, usually, three 40-hour National Units, plus another 40 hours for review and consolidation for an external assessment.

- **Scottish Group Awards (SGAs)** are made up of groupings of National Units and National Courses. They can be taken over one year full-time, or part-time over a longer period.

Scottish Vocational Qualifications (SVQs)

These are the counterpart to NVQs offered elsewhere in the UK, and operate on a similar basis. SVQs are available over a wide range of occupational fields.

Scottish Qualifications Certificate (SQC)

The **Scottish Qualifications Certificate** replaced the Scottish Certificate of Education (SCE) and Record of Education and Training (RET). The Certificate comprises a complete record of a student's achievements, listing all types of qualifications gained. It is designed to be cumulative, so that later qualifications can be added. It includes a core skills profile.

Further information

QCA (Qualifications and Curriculum Authority) – 83 Piccadilly, London W1J 8QA. Tel: 020 7509 5555. Covers England, Wales and Northern Ireland. Information about academic and vocational qualifications can be found on: www.qca.org.uk

SQA (Scottish Qualifications Authority) – based at Ironmills Road, Dalkeith, Midlothian EH22 1LE and at Hanover House, 24 Douglas Street, Glasgow G2 7NQ. Tel: 0845 279 1000. Their website also contains information about qualifications: www.sqa.org.uk

Basic Skills Agency – Commonwealth House, 1-19 New Oxford Street, London WC1A 1NU. Tel: 020 7405 4017. www.basic-skills.co.uk

National Open College Network – 9 St James Court, Friar Gate, Derby DE1 1BT. Tel: 01332 268080. www.nocn.org.uk

The following resources may be available in adult guidance agencies and public reference libraries. The list contains comprehensive reference books and handbooks which are more likely to be found in libraries.

British Qualifications – a reference directory of educational, technical, professional and academic qualifications. Lists qualifications by trades and professions and contains details of professional institutions and accrediting bodies. Published by Kogan Page.

British Vocational Qualifications – comprehensive reference to vocational qualifications. Published by Kogan Page.

NVQs and How to Get Them – published by Kogan Page, £9.99.

How to Choose Your GCSEs – published by Trotman, £12.99.

Which A levels? – published by Lifetime Careers Publishing, £12.99.

University and College Entrance: the Official Guide – published annually by UCAS; lists courses across the UK leading to degrees, HNDs and DipHEs.

Chapter four
Where to learn

All providers of learning opportunities publish a range of information to advertise and describe their courses – both in booklets/information sheets and through websites. It may be easy enough to get hold of such information, at the cost of a few telephone calls or visits to course providers, or spending some time on the internet, but making sense of it all is less easy. Even if you know what type of course you want to do, tracking down the college or training provider that provides exactly what you want, making an application and getting accepted can be a time consuming process.

This chapter provides you with a guide to the different types of learning providers, from adult education services through to universities. It covers what they provide, who to contact for advice and further information and how to apply for courses. It is preceded by more general advice on getting information. The chapter concludes with a word about study and training abroad.

Working through the information maze

There's a lot of information out there – but how do you know where to start looking? It is obviously preferable to target those learning providers that run the sort of courses that you wish to take. But which ones are they?

One short cut is to take advantage of the various agencies that  exist to provide answers to just those sorts of questions!

- **learndirect** is the national telephone helpline for any adult wanting information about learning opportunities of any type; their freephone number is **0800 100 900**. Lines are open from 8.00am to 10.00pm seven days a week. Or you can search for courses through their website: www.learndirect.co.uk If you live in Scotland, tel: 0808 100 9000, Mon-Fri 7.30am to 11pm, Sat/Sun 9am to 6pm. Or view: www.learndirectscotland.com

- **In England, adult information, advice and guidance (IAG) agencies** can provide information and advice, and hold leaflets, prospectuses and course directories, and provide access to databases on learning opportunities locally and nationally. In **Wales** and **Scotland**, adults can find information and help through Careers Wales and Careers Scotland, respectively. See chapter nine for more information about the services available through such organisations.

- Most **public libraries** will have an education section and a noticeboard advertising courses and coming events. They are also likely to have many of the national directories of education and training, and generally offer public internet access.

It is also worth keeping a lookout for any local 'education fairs', 'education and training roadshows' and similar events that may be put on in your locality. These provide an opportunity to talk directly to providers of courses. Local newspapers also sometimes do special features on learning opportunities – especially around the main enrolment season for educational institutions – late August/early September.

With assistance from such sources, you can identify possible courses of interest, and start to make a shortlist of those most likely to be of direct interest. You may live within easy travelling distance of several education and training providers. If you include all local colleges, adult education centres and private education and training organisations, then you may have a wide choice of providers. Do not be discouraged if the first provider you approach cannot deliver the goods. By considering all the options, you greatly increase your chances of finding a suitable course near to you. Even in rural areas, you might be surprised at the number of providers within reachable distance.

An overview of providers

- The major providers of learning opportunities are the **public sector colleges and universities**. They offer a huge range of courses at every level. They receive public funding towards their costs; fees are payable by adult students but some students may get fee remission, or assistance towards their fees – see chapter five.

- A network of **learndirect** open learning centres operate across England and Scotland offering a range of courses through computer-based learning packages.

- There are also **independent providers** of education and training, operating on a commercial basis, although some are registered educational charities. The opportunities provided through the independent, or private, sector also cover a wide range of subject areas, from basic to professional level.

- The Government provides **work-based learning** opportunities for unemployed people. The training is delivered through various agencies, under contract. Many independent learning providers are contracted to provide government-funded training.

- Learning opportunities can also be provided by **voluntary organisations**, and other community based, non-profitmaking bodies.

- **Employers**, of course, provide learning opportunities for their staff; for many employees, this includes the opportunity to gain qualifications.

- Many **professional bodies** offer work-related qualifications for their field of work.

When researching information about learning opportunities, it helps if you are aware of the distinction between further education and higher education:

- **Further education** is learning at non-advanced level i.e. up to level 3 (A level standard) (see page 37). Further education includes courses leading to NVQ and other vocational qualifications, as well as academic courses, up to level 3. Further education courses can be taken on a full- or part-time basis, including through open and distance learning. Further education courses differ enormously in the time they take, from a few weeks to, say, two years.

- **Higher education** is learning at a standard beyond level 3. It embraces diplomas, degrees, professional qualifications and postgraduate awards. Studying for these awards requires a sustained commitment. Most undergraduate degree courses, for example, require three years' full-time study. That does not mean you have to be a full-time student; there are increasing opportunities to study on a part-time basis, but all options will require a substantial investment in time. What can cause confusion is that most further education colleges provide opportunities both at further **and** at higher education level.

The providers

The following providers of education and training are described:

- adult and community education

- voluntary organisations

- Workers' Educational Association (WEA)

- U3A

- learning at work – employers and trade union-based learning

- learndirect centres

- government-funded learning programmes for unemployed adults

- colleges of further education

- adult residential colleges

- universities and colleges of higher education

- the Open University

- independent providers – including independent open/distance learning providers.

Adult and community education

Evening classes or short daytime courses are widely available through adult and community education. A huge range of general interest courses for recreation, leisure and personal development are offered. These include 'return to learn' courses and basic skills courses (literacy and numeracy), GCSE courses and AS and A levels. Basic vocational qualifications may also be on offer.

Adult and community education can be offered through:

- adult and community education centres, run by adult education services of local education authorities

- colleges of further education

- community colleges or community schools

- the extra-mural departments of universities.

The philosophy of adult and community education services is to make courses open and accessible to all. Many services make considerable efforts to provide advice and guidance prior to enrolment, to run crèches and to accommodate the needs of people with disabilities. Booking is made simple, either by telephone, post or by direct application at various centres during enrolment days (or weeks). A policy of 'first come, first served' usually applies.

Overall responsibility for the funding of adult and community education in England is the responsibility of local Learning and Skills Councils. These Councils, in partnership with local education authorities (LEAs), develop future arrangements for adult and community education. Adult and community education operates from a variety of premises, often in local schools, and under a number of identities. To get details for your area, contact your LEA and ask for the department which deals with adult and community education. Your local library and adult information, advice and guidance agency should also be able to advise, of course.

In Wales, ELWa (Education and Learning Wales) takes responsibility for adult and community education, while in Scotland, it is the responsibility of the Scottish Executive (Enterprise, Transport and

Lifelong Learning Department). In Northern Ireland, the Department for Employment and Learning oversees lifelong learning. You can find out more via their websites (listed at the end of this chapter).

Voluntary organisations

Many charities, voluntary bodies and community organisations run education and training courses. For some, such as Shelter, which runs courses for voluntary and statutory workers in housing advice, law, homelessness and welfare benefits, it is a natural extension of their other activities. For others, like the Workers' Educational Association, which is perhaps the best-known voluntary provider, education is the primary activity. Voluntary organisations tend to specialise in particular disciplines or cater for a specific clientele, rather than duplicating the type of courses readily available from colleges, universities or commercial training companies.

Many voluntary bodies provide well-respected training, and for some, such as Relate or the Samaritans, thorough and in-depth training of volunteers is of crucial importance. Increasingly, the training offered through voluntary organisations is becoming formally accredited, often through local Open College Networks (see page 49). Most organisations offer some kind of training, however, many have a precarious future as the sector is heavily dependent on sponsorship, short-term grants and (increasingly limited) local and central government funding. The places to look for information about organisations active in your area are your local volunteer bureau, public libraries, community centres and guidance centres.

Volunteering England – Regent's Wharf, 8 All Saints Street, London N1 9RL. Tel: 0845 305 6979. Publishes information for prospective volunteers, which is available to view on their website: www.volunteering.org.uk

See also: Volunteer Development Scotland at www.vds.org.uk

Wales Council for Voluntary Action: www.wcva.org.uk

Volunteer Devlopment Agency (Northern Ireland): www.volunteering-ni.org

Workers' Educational Association (WEA)

Founded in 1903, the WEA, an independent organisation and a registered charity, provides part-time education for adults. It runs courses both for groups of individuals and for collective bodies such as trade unions, community organisations and women's groups. The association aims to bring education to the widest community, in particular to those who have previously missed out on education.

The WEA is organised on a regional basis, with over 650 branches throughout the UK. It is a democratic body, open to all; members have a say in what courses each branch runs, and students are consulted on course content and teaching methods. Individual course programmes therefore vary from area to area, but typically the programmes fall into three broad areas:

- **The general programme** – run by local branches across the country, and open to all; topics range widely from history or archaeology to creative arts, writing or return to learn. They are usually part-time day or evening courses.

- **The community programme** – courses are designed to meet particular local needs and are delivered in partnership with local groups and voluntary and statutory organisations. Courses are run in particularly disadvantaged areas. Subjects are wide ranging, from return to learn and IT through to health and arts and crafts.

- **Workplace learning** – through linking with trade unions and employers, the WEA delivers a range of courses in the workplace.

Fees usually have to cover the costs of running the course. Courses aimed particularly at those who are unemployed or disadvantaged are usually free.

Detailed information about local WEA activities can be obtained from local branches or regional offices; get contact addresses from libraries or the phone directory, or via their website.

WEA national office – Quick House, 65 Clifton Street, London EC2A 4JE. Tel: 020 775 3092. www.wea.org.uk

U3A

The U3A – University of the Third Age – was started in the UK in1982. It is an organisation created to encourage lifelong learning for those who are no longer in full-time employment. There are currently 540 groups, with over 140,000 members. U3A members organise learning groups themselves, using the skills of the members to organise and teach. The subjects tackled vary according to the interests and skills of the group, and range from local history or foreign languages to computing.

You don't need any qualifications to join a group, and each member pays a small annual membership fee. Your local library should be able to provide contact details of your local group, or consult the U3A website.

U3A National Office – Old Municipal Buildings, 19 East Street, Bromley, BR1 1QH. Tel: 020 8466 6139. www.u3a.org.uk

Learning at work

Much of the learning undertaken by adults relates to their employment, and is supported by their employers. Trade unions also play an important role in developing opportunities for workplace learning. Learning opportunities available range from basic skills through to those at professional level. The Government has placed great emphasis on encouraging employers to provide quality training to their workforce – in order to equip employees with the skills and qualifications needed for a successful future economy.

Employers

Many, particularly larger employers, have well-established staff training and development programmes.

- These may involve employees working towards nationally-recognised qualifications, such as NVQs, which can be gained through assessment in the workplace.

- Employees may follow the traditional pattern of attending part-time courses at local further education colleges – perhaps a half day and evening a week, for example.

- Some staff gain qualifications through distance learning. Such courses may be provided through colleges, universities, independent providers or professional bodies.

- A few employers have learndirect centres (see below) based in their premises, for the benefit of employees.

If you are employed, your employer could support your training through paying your course fees and/or allowing you paid or unpaid time off to attend a course or open learning centre. If you are in work and wish to gain further work-related qualifications, find out from your employer what support may be available. It can also be possible to achieve a higher education qualification whilst working (or self-employed) through an intitiative called Learning through Work (LtW), delivered through learndirect in partnership with certain higher education institutions. You can find out more on the learndirect website: www.learndirect.co.uk

If you are planning a return to work, when looking at job vacancies check what training opportunities may be open to you. There are a few large employers that run employee assistance programmes, not only for work-related courses, but for any learning opportunity of the employee's choice.

Apprenticeships

Apprenticeships (formerly called Modern Apprenticeships) provide work-based learning leading up to NVQ level 3 across a wide range of career areas. Trainees are normally employed. To date, Apprenticeships have been aimed at young people aged up to 25, but this upper age limit is being scrapped by the Government, and Apprenticeship programmes that are appropriate for those aged over 25 are currently being developed by Sector Skills Councils (the bodies that have responsibility for skills development and training in particular occupational areas) and local Learning and Skills Councils.

Trials of Apprenticeships for Adults start from September 2004 in some areas across England, involving up to 1300 learners. These will include those who are employed who have skills but are without qualifications, as well as those who are unemployed or facing unemployment and wanting to change the type of work they do.

In Scotland, there has been no upper age limit for entry to Apprenticeships (although 16/17 year-olds have priority), and in Wales, there is no upper age limit, although access for adults may be determined by the availability of placements. In Wales, the Modern Skills Diploma for Adults is aimed at adults in work who are aged 25 and over, who want to improve their skills and knowledge at NVQ level 3 and above.

Trade union-based learning

Trade unions have long been involved in encouraging employees to develop their skills and qualifications, and in providing learning opportunities. TUC Learning Services has been established to help unions and their members to increase participation in workplace learning. An important element of this has been the setting up of a Union Learning Fund. This finances a huge range of projects within the workplace which increase access to workplace learning, such as the setting up of workplace learning centres, so providing staff easy access to flexible open learning courses.

In addition, a trained network of Union Learning Representatives has been developed, to provide advice and guidance to employees.

There are, therefore, tremendous opportunities for furthering your skills and qualifications through your job, supported by your employer. Don't feel you have to do it all before you enter the workplace!

You can find out more about the role of trades unions in encouraging learning in the workplace on www.learningservices.org.uk

learndirect centres

The first learndirect centres were set up in 1999, and there are currently over 2000 centres across England, Wales and Northern Ireland, and over 400 in Scotland. learndirect centres offer access to learning which is delivered via computers and the internet – i.e. you use a computer to work through a learning package, at times and at a pace that suits you. It is therefore a very flexible way of learning.

learndirect centres are run by a variety of organisations that have contracted to operate them. This includes colleges, employers, voluntary organisations and so on. Centres are based in a variety of settings which are easily accessible to the public, including in community centres, libraries and shopping centres. Some centres are based in companies, for the benefit of their employees. If you have your own computer, it is also possible to undertake learndirect courses through distance learning at home, with online and telephone support from tutors.

There are about 450 courses currently on offer through learndirect centres in England, Wales and Northern Ireland. Courses are delivered online, so you need an internet link, although some may be accessed via a CD-ROM, and paper-based materials and workbooks may be also be used for some courses. Courses cover the following areas: home and office IT; specialist IT; business and management; languages and skills for life (e.g. word and number skills). Courses range from those aimed at people returning to learning through to professional skills courses for those working at management level. The duration of courses varies widely – while between 10 and 20 hours is typical, there are others which take more or less than this. The number and range of courses are increasing all the time.

Some learners may be able to get help towards fees, at the discretion of the particular learning centre. Anyone who is in financial hardship should enquire at their nearest learndirect centre.

To find out about your nearest learndirect centre, and about available courses, telephone the learndirect helpline: 0800 100 900 or if you live in Scotland, tel: 0808 100 9000. Or you can find information on: www.learndirect.co.uk and www.learndirectscotland.com

Government-funded learning programmes for unemployed adults

There are a number of Government-funded training opportunities for unemployed adults operating across the UK. The programmes aim to equip adults with work-related skills and qualifications. Eligibility to join such programmes depends on how long you have been unemployed, or on your personal circumstances. The rules are quite complex, so the starting point for further information on eligibility and what is available in your locality is your local Jobcentre Plus/Jobcentre. The main programmes currently running are described below.

The New Deal

The New Deal is the Government's main programme to help people get back into employment. Under New Deal, there are a number of programmes catering for different groups of people, usually after a certain length of time being unemployed, although some can be offered early entry. There are programmes for young people, for people aged 25 plus, for those aged 50 plus, for lone parents,or those with disabilities and for partners of unemployed people. There are also programmes for those wanting to become self-employed, and for those aiming at a career as a musician.

A variety of options are available under each New Deal programme; all are concerned with helping people to find employment – help with finding and applying for jobs, drawing up an action plan and so on, but included under some programmes are opportunities for skills training.

Under **New Deal for those aged 25 plus**, training that focuses on a specific job, and courses to develop employability skills can be an option for those who are having difficulty finding employment. Eligibility for this programme is normally for those who have been claiming Jobseekers' Allowance (JSA) for at least 18 months. In some cases, earlier entry is possible.

The **New Deal for young people** (i.e. those aged 18-24) is open to those who have been claiming Jobseekers' Allowance for six months or more, although some may enter earlier. Vocational and/or key skills training is an option under this programme.

Work-based Learning for Adults (WBLA)

WBLA is offered in England, through the Department for Work and Pensions. A similar programme is currently available in Wales. In Scotland, **Training for Work** is the equivalent programme, which runs along broadly similar lines, and is the responsibility of Local Enterprise Companies (LECs). In Northern Ireland, the **Training for Work** and **Bridge to Employment** programmes are offered.

Currently, Work-based Learning for Adults is open to people aged over 25, who have been registered unemployed for six months or more. However, various other people who have not been registered as unemployed for this period are also eligible. This includes people with disabilities; returners to the labour market after, for example, looking after a child or other relative; lone parents; those who have lost their job through large-scale redundancy; Armed Forces leavers; and those who need basic skills training in literacy and numeracy or help with spoken English.

Each person joining the programme follows an individual training plan, according to their needs. This could include work experience with an employer, the chance to gain NVQs, job specific training or a mixture of these. Basic employablilty training may be an option for those who need extra help before starting training for a particular job. Help with basic skills (literacy and numeracy) may be included, or help with spoken English, for those for whom English is not their first language.

While on WBLA, you get an allowance equivalent to any benefits you are currently receiving, plus £10 a week. There may also be extra help for travelling expenses or childcare.

Apprenticeships

See above (under Learning at work) for information about possible opportunities for some unemployed people through the new Apprenticeships for Adults trials in England.

To find out more

For information about the range of training opportunities for unemployed people through the New Deal and other programmes, contact your local Jobcentre Plus/Jobcentre.

The Government's New Deal website provides information about the full range of options under New Deal: www.newdeal.gov.uk – the website includes a 'discovery tool' which allows you to find out if you are eligible. You can also telephone the New Deal helpline on 0845 606 2626 (textphone 0845 606 0680).

Richard Griffiths – found a job through work-based learning

Richard's experience of unemployment eventually led him to embark on training which, in turn, launched him into a new career.

'After leaving college, although I was well qualified, I had difficulty finding work due to my lack of work experience. After being unemployed for two years, I was referred to Spring Skills, as part of the Government's Work-Based Learning for Adults scheme. I joined as a trainee; working in the company's IT training room. I was shortly moved to work in the reception area, to gain work experience in administration. Here I was taught general office skills, and how to use the computer system. After two months of intense general office skills, I became employed with Spring Skills as a full-time administrator.

I feel that working at Spring Skills, holding down a responsible position, has boosted my self-confidence tremendously. Receiving a proper salary after being on benefit for some time is another obvious bonus. Whilst working for Spring Skills, I was also offered the chance to gain an NVQ level 3 in business administration, which is sure to help me in the future. Spring Skills gave me great support whilst re-training, and, as a result of my job here, I now have a much wider range of practical skills and experience with which to further my career.'

Colleges of further education

The further education sector is a major provider of education for adults. As mentioned earlier in this chapter, further education comprises education up to level 3, i.e. courses up to A level standard/NVQ level 3. In November 2003, the number of people aged 19+ undertaking further education was 1.56 million – so you would not be alone if you entered further education as an adult!

Most further education colleges run courses across a wide range of subjects leading to academic and vocational qualifications, from basic education and refresher courses in subjects like English and maths, through to courses at higher education level. Some colleges specialise in particular disciplines such as agriculture/land-based courses or art. Many colleges also provide a full programme of leisure and recreational courses for adults.

College names can be confusing because there is no consistency or standard convention. Whether your local college is called Townsville College of Further Education, Townsville College of Arts and Technology, or just plain Townsville College, it is likely to offer much the same broad range of courses. Specialist colleges, such as Townsville College of Art, tend to be self-evident.

Flexibility and ease of access

One of the reasons colleges are successful at attracting large numbers of mature students is because they make a virtue out of being flexible. There has always been a strong tradition of part-time courses in the further education sector. Many courses are run during evenings or on a day-release basis. Modular programmes (see chapter two) enable students to work towards qualifications step by step. In recent years, colleges have made great efforts to reach more people. A range of courses to encourage adults back into education have been offered, such as 'return to learn' and similarly titled courses. Many colleges offer open or flexible learning centres; these are particularly useful if you are unable to attend college on a regular basis, allowing you to follow, at times convenient to you, certain courses via a computer (see chapter two). Other colleges have 'moved into the community', running courses in outstations and community centres. Some have developed courses that are particularly appropriate for those with special needs – with, for example, specialist computing facilities designed for those with particular needs. Most colleges offer crèches and day nurseries. And you don't necessarily have to enrol in September as more courses are now run all year round.

Some courses offered by some colleges may be made available to learners on a distance-learning basis.

Wide range of qualifications

At further education colleges you can study for a wide range of qualifications, both academic and vocational. These include qualifications offered by professional bodies, such as the Chartered Institute of Marketing, Association of Accounting Technicians, or the International Therapy Examination Council.

Routes to higher education

Further education colleges are the major providers of Access courses (see page 42), which prepare adults without formal qualifications for entry to universities and higher education colleges.

FE colleges have always provided a limited range of higher education courses, mostly at Higher National Certificate or Diploma level e.g. HND business or HNC electrical/electronic engineering. In recent years they have increasingly offered study at degree level, and this is set to expand further with the recent introduction of foundation degrees (described more fully on page 46).

Colleges of further education are able to offer degree courses through franchising arrangements with universities. Sometimes the college is able to offer the first year of the degree, sometimes the whole of the degree course. This enables students to take either the first stages of a university course, or the whole of it, at a local college.

This linking of further and higher education institutions can be of huge benefit to adult learners with home and family commitments whose local town does not have a university. Such arrangements can make the difference between higher education being a viable option or not.

Entry requirements to higher education courses are generally flexible for adults. Admissions staff are prepared to take into account previous experience whether it is in (paid or voluntary) work, at home or in education (see accreditation of prior learning, page 47). The test is whether the applicant will benefit from the course, and guidance staff will sometimes recommend preparatory or foundation programmes where appropriate.

To find out more

To find out what your local college can offer, contact their **admissions units**. Most colleges produce separate part- and full-time prospectuses; some produce separate prospectuses listing courses at higher education level. Look also at their websites, which generally offer a course search facility. Some colleges have mature students' advisers (or guidance counsellors) who can advise both on courses and the practicalities of returning to study.

You can also find out about courses both in your local area and further afield by contacting learndirect (or learndirect Scotland) or viewing their websites – see details at the beginning of this chapter.

Course Discover is a searchable database of further and higher education courses in the UK. May be available in information, advice and guidance agencies. Produced by Trotman.

Mature Students' Directory is an annual directory published by Trotman. Covers further and higher education institutions within the UK, providing information on what each offers for mature students.

Adult residential colleges

Adult residential colleges offer an alternative way of returning to academic education and preparing for study at a higher level. They provide a relaxed environment in which to live, work and learn, and they may be particularly, suitable for people who left school early or with few qualifications. There are seven colleges across the UK, each with a distinctive academic programme, although mainly in social sciences and the humanities. In addition to their residential programmes, some of the colleges also run part-time and short courses. The colleges welcome and cater for adults of all ages. There are no formal entry qualifications for most courses; instead, selection is by interview and sometimes some written work.

Adult Education Bursaries are available for full-time residential courses. These cover course fees, provide funding towards living expenses and some assistance with travel expenses. Applicants for bursaries must be at least 20 years old before the start of the academic year in which the course starts. Each college has full details about which courses and which students are eligible for this support. More information about the bursaries is provided in chapter five.

Further information can be obtained directly from each college.

Coleg Harlech WEA offers a nine-month access course in a variety of subject areas, for those wishing to progress to higher education. Contact: Coleg Harlech WEA, Harlech, Gwynedd LL46 2PU. Tel: 01766 780363. www.harlech.ac.uk

Fircroft College runs a one-year access programme, and various short courses. Contact: Fircroft College of Adult Education, 1018 Bristol Road, Selly Oak, Birmingham B29 6LH. Tel: 0121 472 0116. www.fircroft.ac.uk

Hillcroft College is a women-only college, offering a one-year Certificate in Higher Education course, and a variety of other courses. Contact: Hillcroft College, South Bank, Surbiton, Surrey KT6 6DF. Tel: 020 8399 2688. www.hillcroft.ac.uk

Newbattle Abbey College offers a one-year course which is recognised for entry to universities and higher education colleges. Contact: Newbattle Abbey College, Newbattle Road, Dalkeith, Midlothian EH22 3LL. Tel: 0131 663 1921. www.newbattleabbeycollege.co.uk

Northern College's programme includes a full-time, nine-month diploma course (part-time study also possible), which is recognised as a university entrance qualification. The College also offers a Certificate of Higher Education in trade union studies. Various short courses are also available. Contact: Northern College, Wentworth Castle, Stainborough, Barnsley S753ET. Tel: 01226 776000. www.northern.ac.uk

Plater College is a Catholic institution, but welcomes applications from people of other faiths. It runs a one-year Certificate in Higher Education, equivalent to the first year of a degree course. Students follow one of four subject pathway options. Contact: Plater College, Pullens Lane, Oxford OX3 0DT.Tel: 01865 740500. www.plater.ac.uk

Ruskin College offers a Certificate of Higher Education in a variety of subjects. Other courses include a Diploma of Higher Education in social change, a foundation degree in youth and community work and a degree in social work. Contact: Ruskin College, Walton Street, Oxford OXI 2HE. Tel: 01865 310713. www.ruskin.ac.uk

Other residential colleges

There are various short-term residential colleges, offering mainly short leisure courses, in a wide field of subjects, such as in arts and crafts, music, history, natural history etc. For more information, see the publications listed below, or you can view the website of ARCA – the

Adult Residential Colleges Association – an association of around 30 adult residential colleges offering short-stay residential courses: www.aredu.org.uk

Time to Learn – lists residential courses in the UK and overseas. Published twice a year by City and Guilds, tel: 020 7294 2850. Price £4.95 (plus £1.50 p+p). Or view on the website: www.timetolearn.org.uk

The Adult Learning Year Book – published by NIACE, is a directory of organisations and resources in adult continuing education and training, and includes lists of short-term residential colleges. To order, tel: 0116 204 4216. Price £18.95.

Emma Thew – decided to achieve something for herself!

Emma had been working in administrative work before deciding to take the plunge back into full-time education.

'Going to university was something I had thought about for a while. After the birth of my child I felt more than ever that I wanted to do something for myself. As a parent, you want the best for your child and want them to achieve all their goals – and I thought why shouldn't I want the same for myself! I chose history as my main subject as it was something that had always fascinated me, even though I hadn't studied it since taking my GCSEs ten years ago! I applied to several local universities and was fortunate enough to get accepted to all of them. After visiting and studying course prospectuses I decided to accept a place at Bath Spa University College. The campus was beautiful but what really made my mind up was the wide choice of history modules available, which included amongst many others, local history studies.

After contacting my LEA I discovered that, as a single parent, I was entitled to a Childcare Grant that covered 85% of my childcare costs, a full loan, full payment of fees and a Parents' Learning Allowance of over £1300. These, with two part-time jobs and an overdraft, have made studying whilst bringing up a child workable!

My first year at university has been an amazing experience. I have made some great friends and I have learnt many skills that I am proud of, such as how to

accurately research a topic and confidently give a good presentation. Working previously in administration had prepared me for the organisation required to handle my workload, although it had not prepared me for the workload itself! Like everything, everyone has a different way of working and I feel that during this first year I have found mine.

I'm working over the summer now and I can't wait to start my second year in September. I know a lot of people think there are too many obstacles preventing them from going back to full-time education but help is available and with determination and a bit of courage anyone can do it!'

Universities and colleges of higher education

The higher education system has expanded rapidly in recent years, and is set to continue to expand with the Government's aim that 50% of all those aged under 30 should experience higher education. The expansion over the last twenty years or so has included a significant increase in the numbers of mature students. The traditional image of a university as a place for young people attending full-time courses is now out-dated. If you are contemplating higher education as a mature student, you will not be alone!

Several of the profiles included within this book describe the experiences of those who have embarked on higher education as mature students, such as Emma (above), Carole (page 151) and James (page 97) and show vividly the sense of satisfaction and achievement that they experience. Nowadays, in many institutions, the proportion of mature undergraduates is surprisingly high – in fact, the over 25s are the fastest-growing group. The great majority of part-time students are mature, and between a quarter to a third of full-time undergraduates being mature is not unusual in many institutions. However, this proportion does vary tremendously between different institutions, and some still have only a very small proportion of mature students. In 2003, around 23% of students entering full-time higher education were aged 21 or more – that's nearly 120,000 people. Of this group, just over half were aged 21-24 and most of the rest were aged 25-39. While fewer than one in ten was aged 40 or more, that still amounted to over 10,500 people. You will, however, find that mature students are not necessarily evenly spread amongst the different subject areas – typically, more are found on arts and social science courses than science and engineering courses, for example.

The UCAS directory *University & College Entrance: The Official Guide*, cites the overall proportions of mature students on degree and HND courses within each institution.

Along with an expansion of student numbers in recent years, there has also been an increase in the flexibility of courses. This has resulted in much more opportunity to study for a degree on a part-time basis, which is an attractive option to many mature students. Indeed, as mentioned in chapter two, some degree courses can be followed through attending evening classes!

Universities and the other higher education institutions are committed to a policy of widening access; all are prepared to consider, indeed welcome, mature applicants who lack the formal entry requirements. Many HE institutions have mature student societies, which represent the interests of mature students, and provide a contact point for them. You will, of course, usually find crèche facilities available.

What courses are available?

The higher education sector is made up of universities and, perhaps less well known, colleges or institutes of higher education. All these institutions offer courses at 'higher education' level, i.e.:

- **degrees** – leading to BA, BSc, BEd, etc – usually three or four years' full-time, or longer part-time

- **foundation degrees** – recently introduced qualifications, which are available in vocational subjects, and studied over two years, full-time or longer part-time

- **HNDs (Higher National Diplomas)** – two-year, full-time or three-year sandwich (i.e. with a period in industry in the middle) or HNCs (Higher National Certificates) which are normally part-time courses

- **Diplomas of Higher Education** (usually two years full-time) and Certificate in Higher Education (normally one-year, full-time); such courses may also be offered on a part-time basis

- some **professional** qualifications

- **postgraduate** courses.

In addition, many HE institutions run short courses and programmes of adult and continuing education, which can provide a good introduction back into study. N.B. A more comprehensive explanation of the qualifications available at higher education level is given in chapter three.

As has already been discussed, further education colleges also deliver higher education courses, so, besides researching what's on offer at your nearest universities and higher education colleges, check out what your local further education colleges offer. For example, FE colleges are major providers of HND and HNC courses.

Universities have the authority to award their own degrees. They also award degrees offered by colleges of higher education and degrees run at further education colleges. You will find that the degree courses run at your local college are usually awarded by a neighbouring university.

The range of courses offered by higher education institutions varies, for each institution has its own particular history, strengths and traditions. For example, some were formerly teacher training colleges, so teaching and the arts are a strength; others were polytechnics before 1992, so vocational courses are well represented, and strong links with industry may be a feature. Some institutions offer specialist vocational courses which reflect particular industries of the region, developed through links with local companies.

The University of Buckingham may be of particular interest to some mature applicants: this is an independent university which enables students to achieve an honours degree in two years. Entry is possible in September, January and July. Around 65% of the university's students are aged over 21.

Flexibility of learning

Many courses are modular or unit-based – as described in chapter two. This provides a good choice of study options – in many courses, for example, you choose your modules as you progress, gradually shaping your course and building up towards your qualification over time. Modularisation of courses also means that it is easier to offer a part-time route to qualification, as students can build up modules at a pace that suits them. Furthermore, all is not lost if you need to take a break from your course for a period (although, of course, you would need to check out the financial and other implications of such a decision very carefully).

Some courses offered by universities are available through distance learning.

Finding the information

A glance at a higher education course directory or university prospectus will tell you that higher education institutions offer a huge range of courses; Manchester Metropolitan University, for example, offers courses in over100 different subject areas. For ease of reference, most institutions publish a number of guides for prospective students. To find out more about the courses that interest you, it is important to get hold of the right publications. These may include all, or some, of the following:

- **undergraduate prospectus** – full-time (and sandwich) degrees and diplomas

- **part-time prospectus** – which may include short courses

- **postgraduate prospectus** – including both taught masters and research degrees

- **extra-mural studies information** – adult education courses open to the general public

- **course/departmental booklets** – describing individual courses in more depth

- **professional and industrial training portfolio** – short courses for those at work

- **mature students' guide** – advice and information for prospective mature students.

You will also find comprehensive information about courses and other aspects of HE institutions on their websites.

And if you want to speak to someone personally, admissions officers, course tutors and student advisers may be able to give you much more detailed advice and assistance. Do not hesitate to seek such advice; providing such advice is part of the role of these staff, and it is in everyone's interests that you make the right decision about entry.

When considering higher education, bear in mind:

● the choice of qualifications on offer – remember there are courses other than degrees

● the variation of lengths of courses

● the availability of courses on a part-time, or perhaps a distance learning, basis

● the need for self-discipline and motivation – a considerable amount of private research and background reading is expected when following courses at this level.

Most applications for full-time higher education courses are handled by UCAS – the Universities and Colleges Admissions Service. Information about applying through UCAS, together with information about the other applications clearing houses, is described in chapter seven.

Don't get put off if you don't have the stated entry qualifications.........

Remember that course entry requirements may be relaxed for mature students. Course admissions tutors are mainly interested in whether you have the ability to cope with the course. They will therefore be looking at your experience and any other qualifications you have taken. They may also want to know whether you have undertaken any recent study. If they have concerns that you may not be ready for a particular course, they will advise on some preparatory learning that you could do first.

Postgraduate study

There are a huge range of postgraduate courses available; the various awards are described on page 46. Some are taught courses, others are higher degrees offered after undertaking research. Some are vocational, whilst others are academic. While many students follow a full-time programme, many more postgraduate students study part-time. Some courses are available on a distance-learning basis.

For more information on the courses provided through universities and higher education colleges, consult some of the directories, websites and reference books listed below. Many will be available through information, advice and guidance agencies for adults; some may also be available in public reference libraries. Agencies may also provide access to computer databases to help you identify possible courses.

To find out more

UCAS – Rosehill, New Barn Lane, Cheltenham GL52 3LZ. Tel: 01242 1122211 (applicant enquiry line). A huge amount of information, including a course search facility, is available on their website: www.ucas.com

The Mature Student's Guide to Higher Education – available free of charge from UCAS. Essential reading for any prospective mature student. Available from the UCAS Distribution Team. Tel: 01242 544610.

The Mature Students' Directory – an annually-updated directory providing information and advice for would-be students. Published by Trotman, £19.99.

University and College Entrance: The Official Guide – annually published by UCAS, this directory lists all full-time and sandwich higher education courses across the UK. Contains, for each institution, the percentage of mature students.

Directory of University and College Entry – annually published by Trotman, lists full-time higher education courses across the UK, including entry requirements.

Directory of Teacher Training Courses – annually-updated; covers undergraduate, postgraduate and employment-based teacher training courses across the UK. Published by Trotman, £15.99.

CRAC Degree Course Guides – published by Trotman. 20 guides, each covering a different degree discipline. Includes information about who offers the courses, the style and content of courses, entrance requirements and graduate outlook.

The Complete Guides Series – a series covering seven subject areas at higher education level; each includes course characteristics and career prospects. Published by UCAS in association with Trotman.

www.prospects.ac.uk – the graduate careers website which includes details of postgraduate courses. Advice for mature graduate jobseekers can be found by clicking on 'handling discrimination' (under Career centre) the 'mature students'.

www.useyourheadteach.gov.uk – the Teacher Training Agency's website, containing careers and training information on teaching.

The Open University

The Open University is the largest single provider of distance education in the UK. It has an international reputation for providing higher education to adults. Many courses do not require any formal academic qualifications for entry. Though best known for its range of courses leading to first degrees, the Open University offers a variety of programmes. These include:

- general BA or BSc degrees in the arts and sciences, and degrees in particular subject areas

- professional diplomas in areas such as health and social welfare, education and management development

- postgraduate awards such as masters degrees in education and business and other areas

- short courses in a range of areas including the arts, social sciences, IT and science.

The Open University's courses are open to anybody over 18 years of age. There are no entry requirements for the undergraduate degree programmes. They are genuinely open: there are no admission interviews or other formalities, and if you apply early enough then you will get a place.

Undergraduate programmes with the OU

Undergraduate programmes are organised into a series of separate courses, each worth a particular number of credit points – usually 30 or 60. A 30-point course means around eight hours of study a week, a 60-point course takes around 16 hours of study a week, spread over a year. You need 360 points for a degree. There is usually no limit on the amount of time you can take to get a degree.

There is a wide range of subject areas on offer, covering the arts, social sciences, maths, science and technology. If aiming at a general degree, you choose the topics to cover as you go along. If you wish to gain a named subject degree, such as business studies, history, law or psychology, most of your study must be within a specified range of courses.

Students are sent course materials by post; this includes printed materials, and other resources such as special equipment (e.g. home experiment kits), audio and video cassettes or computer software. Completed assignments are sent back to tutors to be marked. Some courses include BBC broadcasts, and many courses have one-week residential summer schools. Most importantly, tutorial support is provided. Tutorial meetings are held at local study centres, and individual forms of communication with the tutor may be available by e.g. email or phone, if tutorials are not offered, or if you are not able to attend.

Students are assessed through marked assignments throughout the course, and by written examinations, held at a local centre.

It can take six years or more to gain a degree. You can get credit for any previous study in higher education, which would reduce the number of courses you need to do. For most students, however, gaining an Open University degree is a long haul – but thousands do it!

Non-degree courses

You do not have to register for a degree or diploma-level qualification to study with the Open University.

There are a range of other courses available, such as:

● Openings courses – available in five subject areas, these give you a taste of OU study, which take about 14 weeks

● short courses – ranging from eight- to 20-week, part-time courses, or one-week full-time residential courses, which can count towards a degree if you decide to continue your studies

● Certificates – the first step to undergraduate-level study.

Applying

You can apply for Open University courses at any time. Degree courses run over a calendar year from February to November; applications for degrees should be in by the end of October of the preceding year. As the number of places available on some courses is limited – and it's first come, first served – for the most popular programmes (such as those in the arts) you would need to apply early.

You can get further information about all courses, and information on fees and financial support from any of the OU's 13 regional centres. Information (including a list of centres) is also available on the OU website: www.open.ac.uk

The regional centres include the following:

The Open University in Wales – 24 Cathedral Road, Cardiff CF11 9SA. Tel: 029 2066 5636

The Open University in Scotland –10 Drumsheugh Gardens, Edinburgh EH3 7QJ. Tel: 0131 226 3851

The Open University in Ireland – 40 University Road, Belfast BT7 1SU. Tel: 028 9024 5025.

For general enquiries, or as a starting point, contact:

The Course Information and Advice Centre – The Open University, PO Box 724, Milton Keynes MK7 6ZS. Tel: 01908 653231.

Information about courses can be found in the OU's *Undergraduate Courses Catalogue*, and the accompanying *Undergraduate Certificates, Diplomas and Degrees Prospectus*, and on: www3.open.ac.ukstepforward

Sarah Valentine – discovering new worlds

Sarah is studying through the OU, and is finding it a rewarding experience.

For 18 years I worked in the IT industry, both in the UK and in Hong Kong. Although things move quickly in that field, my career had drawn me away from the cutting edge of technology and was failing to inspire me. So two years ago I made the decision to resign from my job as IT consultant for a London law firm to find something I could once again be passionate about. Life's too short!!

I have always been interested in the stars; many a night I would walk into the odd lamppost as my head was firmly fixed upwards. But, having left formal education after sixth form, I wasn't sure if it was feasible to plunge straight into a subject that sounded as grand and complex as 'astrophysics', it seemed way out of my league! I also didn't want to move away from home or travel to study.

So I did a little internet research and found the Open University's short courses. I have now taken, and passed, two 10-week courses: Introducing Astronomy and Exploring Mars. These were a great way for me to rediscover learning. The materials were well presented and concepts simply illustrated. Being short courses you can quickly find out if this method of learning suits you. I found that setting my own pace and timetable much less daunting than fitting into a classroom environment. I was even startled to discover that I am good at maths and physics, something that eluded me at school.

I am still at the beginning of my second journey through education, this one taking me further than I have ever been before – to the edges of the universe. I am now taking a longer OU science course which will enable me to continue to study astronomy at a higher level next year and eventually achieve a physical science and astronomy degree which does not seem so daunting now.

My advice to those returning to study is to choose your subject well – enthusiasm really enhances your chances of success. I have also found that approaching your studies as segments of learning helps psychologically. For example, four one-year segments sounds manageable, whereas one four-year course can seem very overwhelming.

Leaving work and embarking on full-time education is not possible for everyone and I am very fortunate to be supported through this interlude in my salaried life by my encouraging husband. But apart from feeling like a frugal student sometimes, I am really enjoying this challenge; it's wonderful to feel mentally stimulated.

Where will this take me? Well, I don't think I will be on the first manned mission to Mars! But maybe I'll be behind the scenes, part of the team that takes that 'second giant step for mankind'!'

Independent providers

There is a variety of independent providers of learning opportunities operating outside the public sector, offering both academic and vocational courses to the public.

- Some providers run on purely commercial lines, others are registered educational charities.

- Some run courses which require attendance at the college/training centre for teaching sessions, others offer distance learning (correspondence), with full tutor back up.

- Courses on offer include GCSE and A level courses and a range of professional and vocational subjects, such as business studies, computing, accountancy or secretarial qualifications. Other subjects such as cookery, interior design and childcare are also available through independent colleges.

- Some of the larger organisations offer a wide range of courses; other smaller providers deliver courses related to a specific occupational area – ranging from porcelain restoration or soft furnishings to business skills, or concentrating on academic qualifications.

Apart from a few larger organisations, most independent providers are smaller than publicly-funded institutions. Many are found in London and the major cities, although you are likely to find some, in particular private colleges running secretarial/office skills courses, based in larger towns. Of course, location of institutions offering distance learning courses is immaterial, as they can cater for students from any geographical area.

The following are well-known providers of distance learning in the independent sector.

The National Extension College (NEC)

The NEC is a charitable trust, which has been in operation over 40 years. It provides over 140 home study courses, both academic and vocational. Courses range from those you can do purely for pleasure, or those that help you to return to learning, through to professional-level courses in a variety of fields. Courses include GCSEs and A levels and courses related to business and management, counselling and health, art and design and creative writing. Students work through learning packages at a time and pace to suit themselves. Students are assigned a personal tutor; contact may be by post, phone or email. Enrolments can be taken at any time of the year.

Contact: Student Advisers, **National Extension College**, The Michael Young Centre, Purbeck Road, Cambridge. Tel freephone: 0800 389 2839, or 01223 400 350. www.nec.ac.uk

The Open College of the Arts (OCA)

The OCA is a charitable trust, offering home study courses in a wide range of subject areas related to the arts, such as art and design, interior design, photography, creative writing and music. No previous experience is necessary. It is possible through your studies to gain credit towards higher education qualifications.

Contact: Registration Dept, **Open College of the Arts**, Freepost SF 10678, Barnsley S75 1BR. Tel freephone: 0800 731 2116, or 01226 730 495. www.oca-uk.com

Standards and accreditation

Standards in the private sector vary and, in general, course fees are higher than in the public sector, but the best colleges offer a good alternative route for adults to gain qualifications. If wanting to take a course which you hope will help you in your career, you should **check that the qualifications offered are nationally recognised**.

Accreditation by one of the bodies listed below assures you that the college meets certain quality standards. However, you will find that some colleges are not accredited (there is no legal requirement for accreditation). They offer courses in all sorts of subjects, and many run good quality courses which offer value for money, although there is no easy way of knowing. So you should take care in checking out such colleges carefully. Firstly, check whether courses lead to nationally-recognised qualifications. You could try to contact former students and seek their views. Most importantly, asking pertinent questions of admissions staff should help give you the information you need.

Ask about:

- the success rates of previous students

- the amount of tutor contact you should expect

- their range of facilities

- how long they have been established

- the credentials of staff

- what organisations they are members of or accredited through.

Many independent colleges are accredited through the **British Accreditation Council for Independent Further and Higher Education** (usually abbreviated to BAC). Accredited Colleges are inspected every five years, and have an interim visit.

BAC – British Accreditation Council for Independent Further and Higher Education – 42 Manchester Street, London W1U 7LW. Tel: 020 7224 5474. Their website lists approximately 150 accredited colleges: www.the-bac.org

Organisations providing distance education and correspondence courses are accredited through the **Open and Distance Learning Quality Council** (ODL QC). The Council publishes a free advisory leaflet called the *Buyer's Guide to Distance Learning* and can supply a list of accredited course providers. The Buyer's Guide can be accessed through their website, which also carries a searchable course database.

ODL QC –16 Park Crescent, London W1 1AH. Tel: 020 7612 7090. www.odlqc.org.uk

The organisations below can also supply information on independent providers.

Association of British Correspondence Colleges (ABCC) – PO Box17926, London SW19 3WB. Tel: 020 8544 9559. The Association consists of over 20 colleges, which comply with the Association's Code of Ethics. www.homestudy.org.uk

The Council for Independent Further Education – a professional association of over 20 independent sixth form and tutorial colleges. While most students at such colleges are aged 16-19 years, mature students are also welcomed. www.cife.org.uk

Study and training abroad

There are opportunities for study and training abroad, particularly within the European Union. Education and training in EU member states is available to UK citizens on the same terms as citizens of that country. Obviously, courses will normally be taught in the language of the host country, so you would need to be sufficiently fluent to cope. There are, of course, many language schools abroad, which offer short intensive courses. Most advertise in the national press.

Higher education abroad: there are opportunities to study for up to a year abroad as part of your UK-based degree course; for some courses, the year abroad forms an integral part of the course. You can also spend from three months to a year abroad as part of your higher education course through the EU's Socrates-Erasmus programme. This programme covers EU (including the new member states joining in

2004) and EEA (European Economic Area) countries, Romania and Bulgaria. Details of study abroad possibilities are provided in some higher education directories and within prospectuses. Further afield, universities and colleges worldwide are keen to attract overseas students. However, fees are likely to be high for overseas students. Contact the Embassy of the country of interest to you, to find out the possibilities.

UK Socrates-Erasmus Council – Research and Development Building, The University, Canterbury CT2 7PD. Tel: 01227 762712. See information on their website: www.erasmus.ac.uk

Vocational training: training in EU states is, in theory, open to all. There is an EU programme, Leonardo da Vinci, which encourages collaboration between organisations involved in vocational training. Organisations, not individuals, apply for funding under the scheme, which can include work placements in companies in European countries. Training elsewhere in the world is hard to come by, as most countries only accept immigrants who have skills and qualifications to offer.

Leonardo da Vinci programme – The British Council, Education and Training Group, 10 Spring Gardens, London SW1A 2BN. Tel: 020 7389 4389. www.leonardo.org.uk

Many information, advice and guidance agencies centres stock *Eurofacts* and *Globalfacts* leaflets, factsheets which include information about study in European and certain English speaking countries worldwide, or offer access to the Exodus database, which contains information on studying in Europe.

Study Abroad – published annually by UNESCO. 2004-05 edition £17.50 plus postage. Available from The Stationery Office, tel: 0870 600 5522.

Eurochoice – a guide to higher education opportunities in Europe. Available online at www.eurochoice.org.uk

For further information

Apart from those books and websites mentioned throughout this chapter, you could consult the following.

Second Chances: a national guide to adult education and training opportunities – published by Lifetime Careers Publishing. Explains the options of how and where to learn, and provides specialist information for particular groups.

Useful websites:

www.dfes.gov.uk – the site of the Department for Education and Skills – links to www.waytolearn.co.uk – a site full of information for adult learners.

www.elwa.org.uk – the site of ELWa (Education and Learning Wales).

www.scotland.gov.uk – Scottish Executive site – click on topics, education and training, life-long learning.

www.delni.gov.uk – information for those living in Northern Ireland.

And finally…..

All learning providers have staff whose role it is to provide information and advice. Some have advisers especially to help adult enquirers. Besides talking to general admissions advisers, you may have specific questions that only the course tutor can answer. Do not hesitate to ask any question you feel you need to know, and persist until you get an answer. In the long run, it is much better for both you and the provider that you should enrol on the right course; to do that, you need all the necessary information.

If you are uncertain about visiting a college, then ask a friend to accompany you for moral support. Many learning providers hold occasional open days (or evenings) for potential mature students. These provide an opportunity to talk informally with tutors. Though obviously restricted to a single institution, open days give you the chance to see some of the facilities and get a feel for the environment.

Chapter five
Paying your way

If you've followed the advice in the previous chapters, you've now got a pretty good idea of the learning programme you wish to follow. Now it's time to look at the costs. All post-compulsory education and training comes with a price tag. Therefore, before taking up a course or training place, you should work out what's it going to cost you and then find out what help is available.

Financial help often depends on a number of factors – particularly the type and level of course you take, your personal circumstances and which part of the UK you live and study in. Information has been included where that difference is of note.

This chapter will make you aware of the kind of costs you may encounter and will provide you with information on the main sources of financial support available. Nothing concerned with student finance

is ever straightforward – the rules and regulations are complex and change frequently. For specific guidance, it's best to seek help from those who have up-to-date knowledge and those who control the purse strings, so see the further sources of information and advice listed throughout this chapter and at the end.

The chapter covers the following topics:

- the costs of learning
- funding for higher education (including tuition fees and student loans)
- funding for further education
- financial support for open and distance learning
- funding for postgraduate studies
- financial support for students with disabilities
- NHS bursaries
- social work bursaries
- financial incentives for trainee teachers
- funding for dance and drama courses
- Adult Education Bursaries
- sponsorships and scholarships
- Careers Development Loans
- funding from charities and educational trusts
- learning whilst on benefits/government-funded programmes
- financial support from trade unions
- funding from employers
- part-time work
- funding for learning overseas.

Learning costs

As an adult learner, you will normally be expected to pay for your course fees. There may be other costs too, so find out about:

- **living expenses**, especially if you have to run a second home

- **hidden charges**: on some courses there are extra payments for registration, exams or assessments, field trips and for the use of specialist equipment; so find out if the fee is inclusive or whether there are extras

- the cost of buying **books and special equipment**; it might be possible to buy second-hand books and/or equipment either from shops or from students a year ahead of you

- **transport costs**

- any **childcare costs** and/or costs for caring for **other dependent relatives**

- **cancellations**: it's worth reading the small print to find out what you might lose if you have to withdraw before starting a course or during its early stages.

The learning provider (university, college etc) can give you some idea about these costs.

Check whether you are eligible for a **concessionary fee** as learning providers have individual policies on charging reduced fees for those on benefits or low incomes. In addition, paying by **instalments** may be an option – if it would suit you, ask whether your payments can be staggered.

Another aspect to consider is the '**opportunity cost**' of studying, i.e. the money you could be earning were you working instead. If you give up a job to return to learning, then you need to assess whether you believe it is worth the loss of income. You may be poorer in the short term, but you could come to value the investment in the future. Mature students rarely regret returning to learning!

'... apart from feeling like a frugal student sometimes, I am really enjoying this challenge; it's wonderful to feel mentally stimulated.'

Higher education

To qualify for financial assistance in higher education, you must normally have been living in the UK, Channel Islands or Isle of Man for three years prior to the start of the academic year in which your course begins (there are a few exceptions). You must also be living in England, Wales, Scotland or Northern Ireland on the first day of the academic year in which the course starts. If you have previously undertaken higher education with assistance from public funds, your entitlement to help with tuition fees may be affected. **N.B. The figures quoted below are for the academic year 2004/05, except where otherwise indicated.**

Tuition fees

N.B. From September 2006, higher-education institutions in England will be allowed to charge students up to £3000 a year for tuition fees. Instead of paying up-front, fees will be paid back through the tax system once you have finished your course. If you are on a low income, the Government will pay a fee contribution. For Welsh students, see: www.learning.wales.gov.uk for information on changes to student funding arrangements.

In the meantime, students on degree, DipHE, HND, foundation degree and other higher-education courses in **England** and **Wales** may be asked to contribute towards their tuition fees. The maximum fee contribution is £1250. The amount you have to contribute will depend on your own income or, depending on your circumstances, that of your family. A large proportion of students do not have to make a contribution towards their fees at all. All students, even if they think they will have to pay the maximum student tuition fee, must apply to their local education authority (LEA) for assessment.

If you are eligible to pay full fees (e.g. because you don't meet the residence criteria or because you have received financial help for a previous course), your university can set their own rates. These can be several thousands of pounds.

If you are a married, 'independent' student (see below), your husband or wife is expected to make a contribution to tuition fees, and possibly living costs, if their residual income (that's the income remaining after certain deductions from their gross income) is £21,475 or more a year. There is a sliding scale of increasing contributions. If you are an independent student over 25, your partner's income may be assessed in a similar way.

To qualify for **independent status** you normally have to meet one of the following conditions:

● be aged 25 or over before the start of the academic year

● have been married before the start of the academic year for which you are applying for support

● have supported yourself for at least three years before the start of the academic year of the course.

If you don't qualify as an independent student, you partner or parent/s will be expected to make a contribution if their residual income is £21,475 or more a year. If your parent/s or partner earns over £31,973 a year, you will have to pay the fee in full.

The Government has introducing a new package of support for **part-time students**. This includes a **fee grant** of up to £575 if your income is below a certain threshold and if you are studying the equivalent of at least 50% of a full-time course.

If you live in **Scotland** you do not pay tuition fees. Instead, you may have to contribute just over £2000 as a **Graduate Endowment** when you complete your learning. However, if you are classed as a mature student at the start of the course (or if you are a lone parent or have a disability), you are not liable to pay the Endowment.

Student loans

The main source of funding for living costs for students on full-time courses is a student loan. The loans have an interest rate linked to inflation so that, in real terms, you won't pay back more than you borrowed. In England and Wales, 75% of the maximum loan is available to all students under the age of 50, and to those aged 50-54 who intend to return to work after studying. How much of the remaining quarter of the loan you can claim will depend on your income, and/or that of your family. Your LEA will confirm the amount of loan you are entitled to and you then tell the Student Loans Company how much of the loan you want. The maximum loan available for a student in England or Wales living away from home, and not studying in London, is £4095, or if living at home is £3240 (slightly less for the final year).

> '*I am not... looking forward to how I will finance myself as a student, living on a student loan. Returning to study may mean a lack of money, as it can be difficult to find an employer who can offer you work which fits around college hours.*'

Repaying the loan

- From the April after you have finished or left your course, if your income rises above a threshold of £10,000 (this is being raised to £15,000 from April 2005), you will begin to repay your loan.

- If your income falls below the threshold level, your repayments will be suspended.

- For most borrowers, repayments will be paid through the Inland Revenue. If you are self-employed, you will repay the loan through the tax self-assessment system.

- There is no fixed time limit for repayment.

N.B. For the first four years of a medicine or dentistry course, the financial arrangements described above apply. For year five and beyond, you may be eligible for an NHS bursary (see page 106) and help with your tuition fees.

Other financial support

'After contacting my LEA I discovered that, as a single parent, I was entitled to a Childcare Grant that covered 85% of my childcare costs, a full loan, full payment of fees and a Parents' Learning Allowance of over £1300. These, with two part-time jobs and an overdraft, have made studying whilst bringing up a child workable!'

In addition to help with paying tuition fees and access to student loans etc, there is a range of extra financial support.

In **England and Wales**, non-repayable, means-tested **Higher Education Grants** have been introduced. These provide up to £1000 to help with living and studying expenses. In addition, there is a non-repayable **course grant** of £250 for books, travel and course expenditure for part-time students who are on a low income.

> **From September 2006 in England,** universities will only be allowed to charge more than the 'standard tuition fee' of around £1200 if they set out how they will improve access (including financial support) to students from low-income backgrounds. A means-tested, non-repayable **maintenance grant** of up to £2700 (which includes £1200 in fee remission plus the £1000 Higher Education Grant) is to be introduced in 2006. (If you start university before 2006, you will still be eligible for the Higher Education grant mentioned above.) If you are on a full-time course charging the full £3000 a year and you are getting the full £2700 maintenance grant, you will get at least an extra £300 a year in extra financial support, most probably in the form of a **bursary**. So, it will be possible to receive at least £3000 a year in non-repayable financial support.

The **Access to Learning Fund** has replaced access and hardship funds in **England**. Full- and part-time students who need extra money for their course in order to stay in higher education, can apply for help from the Fund through their higher-education institution.

There are other sources of means-tested financial support in **England and Wales**. You should apply through your LEA for the following: the

Adult Dependants' Grant (provides up to £2335 a year for full-time students who have dependant adults); **Childcare Grant** (provides full-time students with up to £114.75 a week for one child, or £170 a week for two or more children, for registered and approved childcare) and the **Parents' Learning Allowance** (a maximum of £1330 a year is paid to help full-time students with children with their course-related costs – more money goes to lone parents and those with more than one child). In addition, **Child Tax Credit** is available from the Inland Revenue – the amount varies depending on your circumstances – see www.inlandrevenue.gov.uk/taxcredits for details.

In **Wales**, students can apply through their LEA for the means-tested **Assembly Learning Grant** of up to £1500 per year (see page 100 for more details). Also in Wales, the funds available through institutions to help students facing financial hardship are called **Financial Contingency Funds**.

In **Scotland**, mature students can apply to their college or university for support from the **Mature Student's Bursary Fund** (subject to eligibility criteria). This is intended to help students with childcare costs etc. **Supplementary grants** are also available to help students with particular needs, such as lone parents.

In **Northern Ireland**, students from low-income households can apply for a non-repayable, means-tested **higher education bursary** of up to £2000 per year.

To find out more

Student Loans Company – enquiry line: 0800 40 50 10. www.slc.co.uk and www.studentfinancedirect.co.uk

Student Support Information Line – 0800 731 9133 or textphone 0800 328 8988. Can provide information about student support in higher education in England and Wales, and copies of the booklets, *Financial Support for Higher Education Students* (gives details on tuition fee support, loans etc) and *Childcare grant and other support for student parents in higher education* – both published by the Department for Education and Skills (DfES). Also on: www.dfes.gov.uk/studentsupport

Students Awards Agency for Scotland – Gyleview House, 3 Redheughs Rigg, South Gyle, Edinburgh EH12 9HH. Tel: 0845 111 1711. Contact for the booklet, *Guide to Student Support*. www.saas.gov.uk and www.fundingforlearners.co.uk

Student Support Branch, **Department for Employment and Learning for Northern Ireland** – Adelaide House, 39-49 Adelaide Street, Belfast BT2 8FD. Tel: 028 9025 7710. www.delni.gov.uk/studentsupport Contact for the booklet, *Financial Support for Higher Education Students.* You can also contact your local Education and Library Board for information.

Students' Money Matters – published by Trotman, £14.99.

Higher Education – the money guide for lone parents – published by One Parent Families (information applies to England and Wales); first copy free to lone parents, otherwise £2.50. Tel: 0800 018 5026 for a copy.

James Bawn – surveying his future

James decided to go back to learning in order to get more out of life. He managed to get financial help from a range of sources.

'Until February 1999, I was running my own business, set up with a grant from the Prince's Trust, selling animal food wholesale. I was working alone, doing long hours, and although the business was doing well, it wasn't exactly what I wanted to do. To be honest, I was bored. One of my mates felt the same, so we decided to chuck it all in, and take a year out in Australia, travelling around and working.

I grew up a lot in Australia, and sorted a lot of stuff out in my head. I decided that although having my own business was good, I wanted more from my life. I was used to physical work (labouring on a building site in Oz, and working in a foundry owned by my family) but I'd never done amazingly at school. After getting a few GCSEs, I went to a local college to do a BTEC first diploma in engineering, but to be honest, I enjoyed the social life more than the course. I even started a City & Guilds in welding and fabrication, but gave that up. I wasn't exactly what you'd call a motivated student!

While I was in Australia, a friend back at home was just finishing a degree in building surveying at the University of Glamorgan, and he recommended me to the course tutor. He got me an interview there, and I was given a place on the degree course starting in 2000. It all happened so fast – one minute I was backpacking around Australia, the next I was signing away the next four years of my life!

Learning the second time around was, surprisingly, a lot easier. I think that I was actually ready to learn. I wanted to prove to people that I wasn't a doughnut and that I could progress. It also helped that I had a genuine interest in the subject I had chosen. Initially, I had thought about going into computers, but as I had worked in the building industry at the lowest level, this really helped me decide that building surveying would interest me more. Doing a degree gave me a direction in my life.

During my course I lived at home, which was tough as a mature student, as I was used to coming and going as I pleased, but it had obvious financial benefits. On top of that, my Dad made sure that I made use of all the financial help available, and I got a student loan and help from the hardship fund.

I found some of the aspects of going back to learning difficult, especially report writing and research because I'd never bothered doing them before – I mean, when I did my BTEC course, I didn't even know where the college library was!

I spent my third year on a sandwich placement, working for a large firm which deals with estate and project management. The pay wasn't great, but the experience was invaluable, and I found that I could apply the skills I had learned on the course to 'real' situations with clients and contractors. And the company obviously liked me, because they asked me to stay on and work for them during my final year…which obviously helped my bank account!

Now, I've just graduated with a 2:1, and have two years' experience of a job as well. I feel like I've achieved something; something that I can be proud of. When I look back at the year I spent sitting in that warehouse, surrounded by animal feed, I can hardly believe how far I've come.'

Further education

Further-education courses are those that go up to advanced level (e.g. AS/A levels, BTEC Nationals and NVQs/SVQs level 3).

In **England, Wales and Northern Ireland**, if you are aged 19 or over, you are normally liable for paying course fees. However, in **Scotland**, full-time further-education fees (and some part-time) are paid through the **Fee Waiver Scheme**. For Scottish further-education funding details, the learning provider you are interested in should be able to advise you.

Where fees have to be paid, most further-education colleges have a flexible fee structure for their courses with a range of concessions for those on benefits. Basic education is normally free, as are courses for English as a second language. Most learning providers quote fees on an annual basis, though some allow you to pay in instalments.

Annual full-rate fees for full-time academic and vocational courses range from about £650 to £800. Annual fees for part-time, day-release courses range from £350 to £600+, though often with substantial reductions for benefit claimants. 'Drop-in' centres for learning ICT, office skills etc charge by the hour (usually between £3 to £5). For an evening course – for example an AS level taught one evening a week over an academic year – expect a fee of around £80 to £150. For recreational education, expect to pay anything between £2.00 and £4.50 per hour. So, for a two-hour course over ten weeks, fees range between £40 and £90. Fees are usually payable either each term or at the outset of the course. Do check with the education provider concerned for exact costs as they can vary widely.

Some colleges choose to charge a nominal fee only for adults on full-time courses; it's well worth 'shopping around' colleges within your reach. Private education and training providers charge what they feel the market will bear; voluntary organisations are likely to set fees to just cover costs. In general, fees will vary according to the particular learning provider, the length of the course and the type of course (with those involving special equipment, laboratory or workshop facilities usually costing more).

N.B. At the time of writing, the Government's Skills Strategy White Paper proposes that all adults in England who lack a level 2 qualification (equivalent to five GCSEs at A*-C) should be entitled to free learning to achieve this.

Other financial support

As a further-education student, there are a number of ways by which you can get extra financial help if you need it. **Learner Support Funds** are administered by colleges in **England** for their own students (both full- and part-time) who are on low incomes or in particular need. The money can be used towards any study costs. There may also be help with **childcare** – colleges get funding so that they can provide free or subsidised nursery places for the children of students on benefits or low incomes. Also, if your course requires that you are **resident**, you may be able to get financial help through your college. **Adult Learning Grants** are being piloted in England. They are means-tested allowances of up to £30 a week for at least two years for those aged 19 to 30 who are studying for their first level 2 or level 3 qualification.

In **Wales**, there is similar financial support for further-education students. If you are a full-time, or part-time, further-education (or higher-education) student in Wales, you can apply through your LEA for a means-tested **Assembly Learning Grant** of up to £1500 a year. The Grant will help with the cost of your books, equipment, travel and childcare costs. For more information, see www.learning.wales.gov.uk

Individual Learning Accounts Wales can provide part-time students (and those doing open and distance learning) with from £100 to £200 towards the cost of a course, depending on your personal circumstances and the course costs. They are targeted at adults with no qualifications or with level 2 qualifications or below. View: www.ilawales.com for further information.

In Wales, **Financial Contingency Funds** are the equivalent of Learner Support Funds in England – they provide support to students facing particular hardship.

If you attend a further-education college in **Scotland**, you can apply to the college for **means-tested support**. The support can help with maintenance costs, support for those with dependants, study and travel expenses etc. **Hardship funds** are provided by the Scottish Executive and distributed by colleges to students if they face financial problems which could prevent them accessing further education. **Childcare support** is also available through colleges aimed mainly at part-time students. Extra childcare funding targets, in particular, the needs of **lone parent students**.

Individual Learning Accounts Scotland were due to be launched in summer 2004. If your income is less that £15,000, you will be able to claim up to £200. A universal scheme will be introduced in 2005 focusing on basic and ICT skills. Information is available from learndirect Scotland (see page 117).

If you are over 19 and a full-time student in **Northern Ireland** taking a vocational course up to NVQ level 3, you can apply for a means-tested **Further Education Bursary** of up to £2000. You should apply through your local Education and Library Board.

To find out more

Look at college prospectuses and websites – they usually provide information about fees and financial support.

Money to Learn – a free DfES booklet on adult further education. Tel: 0845 60 222 60 (quote reference MTLC), or see: www.lifelonglearning.co.uk/moneytolearn

For information about student funding in Northern Ireland, contact DELNI (details under Higher education).

For information about funding in Wales, see: www.elwa.org.uk (the booklet, *Making Learning Work for You: Guide to Funding* can be accessed from this site).

For information about funding in Scotland, see: www.fundingforlearners.co.uk

Further Education – the money guide for lone parents – published by One Parent Families (information applies to England and Wales); first copy free to lone parents, otherwise £2.50. Tel: 0800 018 5026 for a copy.

Janet Namusoke – fulfilling her dreams

Janet is currently studying pattern cutting at an adult college, having successfully completed a course in administration.

'*I left university in 1996 with a degree in political science and German language. However, with no professional qualifications I found it quite difficult to get employment. After three years of odd jobs here and there, and quite a few dead ends in my search for work, I decided to leave my home country, relocate to England and start afresh.*

I found work as a waitress with a hospitality agency while I carried out research on adult education. This research led me to a college where I enrolled to study, and consequently achieve, an NVQ in administration. To go to college I had to cut down on my working hours with the agency. This proved financially challenging as I was barely getting by, what with fees to pay, a roof to keep over my head and food to buy. I was able to overcome this when I got a small, but much needed grant, that I put towards the tuition fees, and I found a permanent evening position as a catering assistant for a law-firm restaurant. The job security and reasonable income gave me peace of mind and I was able to put 100% effort into my studies.

The combination of college work during the day and a job in the evenings was quite a lot to take on and there were moments when I wanted to stop, buy a winter duvet, go to a very quiet corner, lie down and not get up!

Well, I did not buy that duvet and I successfully completed my course and now work as an assistant administrator for a large organisation.

*Coming back to learning has opened doors to other possibilities and opportunities – financially, intellectually and socially – that were closed to me in the past. It has helped improve my self-esteem, and taught me to pay **no** attention to discouragement and disillusionment from within or without. It has also made me realise that with the right ingredients, the sky is indeed the limit. I am currently fulfilling my dream of becoming a skilled fashion designer by taking a course in pattern cutting.*

My advice to all those out there considering a back-to-learning experience? Go for it!'

Open and distance learning

Open or distance learning packages, while very convenient for those who can only study at home, are not cheap. Prices vary enormously depending upon the type of package, the amount of support material provided and the quality of tutorial support and back up. The following (2004) prices give some idea of fee levels – you can normally pay in instalments.

The **National Extension College** (NEC) charges £275 for a GCSE course, £210 for an AS level, £150 for an A2 or £325 for the full A level. See www.nec.ac.uk for more information about NEC fees, special offers and other sources of funding.

Open College of the Arts courses are normally £365 or £485. See www.oca-uk.com for more information.

Open University (OU) fees vary from course to course. Just as an example, you would pay £475 for a level 1 science course, worth 60 points towards a 360 point bachelor's degree. Fees normally include the cost of residential schools, if applicable, and the cost of most learning materials, tuition and assessment. If you cannot afford to pay the fees in one go, you can charge your fees to an **Open University Student Budget Account** so that you can pay in instalments. The OU has its own **Financial Award Fund** and receives extra funding from the Government to assist certain students e.g. those on benefits or on low incomes. A booklet giving a comprehensive listing of sources of assistance, grants and awards for its students, *Financial Support for Open University Study*, may be obtained free of charge from the OU's regional centres. More information about the OU can be found on: www.open.ac.uk

Most **learndirect** courses are offered at both a full and a reduced, government-funded price. You can complete a form on the website (www.learndirect.co.uk) to find out if you are eligible for the reduced price.

Postgraduate studies

Most of the available funding for postgraduate education and training comes from the seven government-funded **Research Councils** and the **Arts and Humanities Research Board** (which is due to become a Research Council). Which organisation funds what depends on the subject area. For instance, the Medical Research Council funds study in the biomedical field and the Economic and Social Research Council funds areas such as economics and social studies. The Arts and Humanities Research Board funds a range of arts and humanities courses. See www.rcuk.ac.uk for further information on all these bodies.

Competition for awards from the Research Councils is very fierce. Awards are usually made on a competitive basis through the university or college concerned. A minimum of an upper second-class honours degree is usually required. You will need to take time and care over your application.

Many postgraduate courses are offered on a part-time basis – perhaps through distance learning – so that coursework and study may be fitted around paid employment. Some other possible sources of funding for postgraduates are listed below. University careers offices will be able to advise you.

- You could consider **a Career Development Loan** if the course is vocational.

- For business administration courses, the Association of MBAs runs the **MBA Loan Scheme**, financed through NatWest Bank.

- Some banks run **other loan schemes** for students on certain courses, such as law.

- You could apply for financial help from the **Access to Learning Fund** (or other similar funds in different parts of the UK) offered by your chosen university.

- A **paid research or teaching assistantship** may allow you to undertake postgraduate study.

- Some grants are available from **charities and trusts**, but these are unlikely to cover the full costs.

- Employers may offer **sponsorship** as part of your career development.

- You could apply for a **scholarship or bursary** for research offered by a university, with money coming from contractual work for industry and commerce, or from university trust funds.

- Some courses attract **commercial sponsorship**.

- Your **family members** may offer the best rates of interest on a loan!

In **Scotland**, the **Postgraduate Students' Allowances Scheme** funds a number of awards on a quota system for places on certain vocational courses. Students are nominated by their university. There are also some awards for non-quota postgraduate courses in areas such as ICT, librarianship and theology. If you are a student in Scotland, see *A Guide for Postgraduate Students* which is also available on: www.saas.gov.uk

Residents of **Northern Ireland** can obtain the booklet, *Awards for Postgraduate Study* from the Student Support Branch of the DELNI (see contact details on page 97).

The Grants Register – The Complete Guide to Postgraduate Funding Worldwide – published by Palgrave Macmillan.

Prospects Postgraduate Funding Guide – published by Graduate Prospects, price £4.99. Information on postgraduate funding can also be found on: www.prospects.ac.uk

Students with disabilities

Some extra help is available if you are a student with a disability. This may include assistance for specialist equipment, help with transport and fee waivers, or reductions, in some cases.

If you take a higher-education course and you have a disability, you may be entitled to the **Disabled Students' Allowance (DSA)**, which is paid through your LEA. DSAs are not means-tested. They are intended to cover any extra costs you have as a student because of your disability e.g. for specialist equipment and non-medical helpers, such as sign-language interpreters. They are not intended to meet costs which you would still incur if you were not a student. Your LEA or the DfES (tel: 0800 731 9133) can provide a leaflet called *Bridging the Gap*.

Funding for Disabled Students in Higher Education; Funding for Disabled Students in Further Education; Applying for the Disabled Students' Allowance; Funding for Disabled Learners from Scotland – and other publications can be downloaded from **Skill**'s website or can be ordered free (if you have a disability) from Skill's Information Service, tel: 0800 328 5050 (textphone: 0800 068 2422). www.skill.org.uk (website has links to Skill Scotland and Skill Northern Ireland).

NHS bursaries

NHS-funded places are available on pre-registration courses in physiotherapy, occupational therapy, orthoptics, radiography, nursing and midwifery, speech and language therapy, chiropody, dietetics, dental hygiene, dental therapy, prosthetics and orthotics, recognised audiology/ hearing therapy courses, operating department practice (diploma course) and medicine and dentistry (in the latter years of pre-registration training). Financial assistance comprises course fees paid by the NHS, a means-tested bursary (or non-means-tested bursary for students on nursing and midwifery diploma courses in England, Wales and Northern Ireland), and access to student loans for the balance of your living costs (for undergraduates only). You can also claim a childcare allowance for up to 85% of your childcare costs. Tel: 0845 009 2559 for information.

N.B. Not all places are NHS-funded. Students who do not receive NHS funds have the same entitlements to loans and help with tuition fees as other higher-education students.

The booklet, *Financial Help for Health Care Students* is available by calling NHS Careers on: 0845 60 60 655, or view: www.dh.gov.uk (click on 'NHS Bursary Scheme' in the A-Z index).

Contact the following for information NHS bursaries in different areas of the UK:

England – NHS Student Grants Unit, tel: 01253 655655

Wales – NHS (Wales) Student Awards Unit, tel: 029 2026 1495

Scotland – The Student Awards Agency for Scotland (see contact details on page 97)

Northern Ireland – contact your local Education and Library Board.

Social work bursaries

If you decide to take a professional qualification in social work, depending on which type of course you do and where you live/study in the UK, you may be eligible for a social work bursary and payment of your course fees. The bursary is worth around £3000 a year. Information can be found on: www.gscc.org.uk/bursaries.htm

Teacher training

Various measures have been introduced to make teacher training an attractive option in areas of the country where there are teacher shortages. Students on postgraduate initial teacher training courses in England and Wales are paid a **training bursary/grant** of £6000 during training, and have their fees paid. If you train through an **employment-based route**, your training will be funded and you will be paid by your employer. The **'fast track'** scheme offers accelerated career progression and offers a bursary of £5000.

If you train to teach a shortage subject in England, you may be eligible for extra funding through the **Secondary Shortage Subject Scheme**. Depending on your financial need, you can be awarded up to £5000 a year (£7500 if you are over 25). In addition, if you teach a shortage subject in England and Wales, you will receive a £4000 **teaching grant** when you start your second year of teaching. The **Payment of Teachers' Loans Scheme** is being piloted in England and Wales until June 2005. Under the scheme, newly-qualified teachers have their student loans paid off over a period of time if they are employed to teach a shortage subject.

If you train to teach in a secondary school in Wales, you may be eligible for a **Secondary Undergraduate Placement Grant** which offers £1000 if you take an undergraduate teacher training course in a secondary shortage subject, and £600 for those training to teach other subjects. The grant is intended to pay for school-based placements. In addition, the **Assembly Learning Grant** is available (see page 100). If you take a secondary PGCE through the medium of Welsh, you may be entitled to the **Welsh Medium Incentive Supplement** which pays £1200.

In England, recruitment incentives ('golden hellos') can give new teachers in certain shortage subjects in **higher education** around £9000 spread over three years. A similar scheme operates for new **further-education** lecturers in shortage subjects who get up to £4000.

For more information, call the Teaching Information Line: 0845 6000 991, or view: www.useyourheadteach.gov.uk. For a brochure on teaching in Scotland, tel: 0845 345 4745.

Dance and drama courses

Dance and Drama Awards give financial support for students on approved dance and drama courses at further-education level at private colleges in England. These awards provide help with fees and living costs for talented students. If you are successful in achieving a Dance and Drama Award (you have to audition for funded places), you will pay no more than £1150 (for 2004/05) towards the cost of your fees. Further information is in the booklet *The Dance and Drama Awards* – phone the DfES publication line on 0845 60 222 60, quoting reference D4. See also: www.dfes.gov.uk/financialhelp/dancedrama

From 2004/05, students entering dance and drama courses at higher-education level at a number of private colleges will be funded in the same way as students in publicly-funded higher education.

If you take a further- or higher-education course in dance or drama in the public sector, you will have access to the same funding arrangements as students of other subjects.

Adult Education Bursaries

Students accepted on to a course at one of the long-term adult residential colleges in England, Scotland and Wales (described in chapter four) may be eligible for an Adult Education Bursary which includes:

- payment of tuition fees

- a means-tested maintenance grant (e.g. of £3335 in 2004/05 for students living in college outside London), plus certain additional allowances

- in some cases, travelling costs in excess of £80 a year.

The bursaries for residents in England and Wales are administered by the residential colleges through their awards offices. In addition, other grants may be available e.g. for students with dependants and for students with disabilities.

Adult Education Bursaries – an annually-published booklet which provides information for English and Welsh residents who wish to study in England and at Newbattle Abbey College in Scotland. Available from the Awards Officer, Adult Education Bursaries, c/o Ruskin College, Walton Street, Oxford OX1 2HE. Tel: 01865 556360.

If you want to study at Coleg Harlech in Wales, contact the college itself on 01766 780363. For Scottish residents, contact the Student Awards Agency for Scotland (see contact details on page 97).

Sponsorships and scholarships

Some employers and other organisations sponsor students in higher education. You normally need to be taking a vocational course related to science, engineering or business. Sponsorship for arts courses is rare. You may be offered a bursary, guaranteed vacation work and/or work experience during a sandwich year. If you obtain such funding, unless it's very generous, it should not affect your entitlement to assistance from public funds.

Scholarships are provided by various bodies e.g. universities and colleges.

They offer a small amount of extra financial assistance to students. Competition for scholarships can be fierce.

You can search for awards on: www.studentmoney.org

University Scholarships and Awards – published by Trotman, £19.99.

Everything You Wanted to Know About Sponsorship, Placements and Graduate Opportunities – published by the British Association with Amoeba Publications, £14.95. Available from Trotman.

Scholarships and Bursaries – published by ISCO, £7.95.

The Offical UK Student Funding Directory – published by Hotcourses Ltd, £9.99.

Career Development Loans

Career Development Loans (CDLs) are available to students and trainees on work-related courses at all levels. Your study can be full-time, part-time or by distance learning. The course must be vocational, and last no more than two years (plus up to a year's work experience if it is part of the course). You can also use the loan to pay for 24 months of a longer course. You are not entitled to a loan if you are receiving financial support from another source. However, a CDL can be used to supplement a bursary or grant that does not cover the full learning costs. You should intend to make use of your learning by working in the UK or elsewhere in the EU or European Economic Area.

You can apply to borrow between £300 and £8000 to cover up to 80% of your course fees, plus the full costs of books, materials and other course costs, including, in some cases, living expenses if you are on a full-time course. If you have been unemployed for three months or longer, you may be able to get a loan to cover 100% of your course fees (your application must be endorsed by your learning provider).

CDLs are available from the Royal Bank of Scotland, Barclays and the Co-operative banks. They will check your credit rating and may refuse applications. You repay the loan at a fixed rate and you do not start to pay it back until up to a month after you complete your course, over a period agreed with the bank. Repayment may be deferred for longer if you are unemployed and/or in receipt of benefits. CDLs are attractive because the interest on the loan is paid for you by the DfES while you are learning. Also, the 'interest holiday' means that the loans are a cheaper source of finance than taking out a personal bank loan or running up an overdraft.

An information pack and application form can be obtained by ringing free on 0800 585 505. Information is also on: www.lifelonglearning.co.uk/cdl

Charities and educational trusts

Numerous educational trusts and charities can provide an additional source of finance for learning. However, any grant is usually small and may only be available if you have exhausted all other possible sources of financial support.

Some general points to bear in mind

- Educational trust funds have strict terms of reference which they have to follow.

- Many funds are available just to support residents of a particular locality.

- Some funds offer assistance only in relation to a specific area of study – such as agriculture or music.

- Upper age limits are frequently cited, which can rule out prospective mature students.

- Financial help may only be available for expenditure on particular items – like books and equipment or childcare costs.

- Assistance is not usually available for study at private institutions.

- Funds may be in the form of a grant or a loan.

Ask the student support department of your LEA or your chosen learning provider for a list of educational charities and trusts. Certainly, seek information and advice from your local adult information, advice and guidance agency.

Once you have identified a fund that might be applicable to you, check carefully the terms of reference and closing dates for application. Apply to the trust fund as early as possible – some require you to apply a year before you intend to commence your education or training course.

The Educational Grants Advisory Service (EGAS) offers guidance, advice and information about sources of financial assistance for learning, including loans, grants, hardship funds, benefits, bursaries and charitable trusts. Services are free to individual students. Advisers at EGAS are experienced at helping mature students and those returning to education. They are particularly concerned with disadvantaged students such as lone parents, people with disabilities, asylum seekers and those on a low income.

The Educational Grants Advisory Service (EGAS) – 501-5 Kingsland Road, London E8 4AU. Tel: 020 7254 6251 (helpline open Mondays, Wednesdays and Fridays from 10am-12noon and 2pm-4pm). www.egas-online.org.uk

The Educational Grants Directory – published by the Directory of Social Change (2004/05 edition out November 2004). A guide to the sources of funding available to students in need, listing trusts and foundations. Covers courses up to and including first degree level.

Charities Digest – published by Waterlow Professional Publishing, Paulton House, 8 Shepherdess Walk, London N1 7LB. Tel: 020 7324 2344. Provides details and addresses of national and regional charities in the UK, including organisations which offer financial help to students and trainees.

Directory of Grant-Making Trusts – available from Trotman.

Learning whilst on benefits/ government-funded programmes

If you live in England or Wales and you have been unemployed for over six months (less in some cases), you become eligible for the **Work-based Learning for Adults** programme. Similar programmes operate in other parts of the UK (i.e. **Training for Work** in Scotland and **Focus for Work** in Northern Ireland). All these programmes are designed to help you back to work through a mixture of training and work experience. In addition, various **New Deal** programmes are also available and these include education and training options.

If you are on a government-funded learning programme, any education or training fees are paid for you. In addition, you normally receive the equivalent of your benefits, plus a small, extra amount (£10 a week for Work-based Learning for Adults), and possibly a contribution towards your travel and childcare expenses. The various government-funded programmes are described fully in chapter four.

Full-time students

In general, if you are a full-time student, you will not be eligible for Jobseeker's Allowance (JSA), Income Support or Housing Benefit. However, full-time students do not normally pay Council Tax.

Some categories of full-time students may still be entitled to claim. The keyword is 'may' – benefit regulations are extremely complex and often depend on your individual circumstances. You will need to get expert advice from your local Jobcentre Plus/Jobcentre, social security office, students' union or Citizens Advice Bureau. Those who may be able to claim one or more benefits whilst learning include:

● lone parents

● students with disabilities (some state benefits, such as Income Support, that are not generally available for full-time students, may be accessible for students with disabilities)

● people who have been unemployed for two years or longer

● student couples with dependant children (during the summer vacation they can claim JSA)

● students on Open University and other distance-learning courses.

Part-time students

If you are unemployed and want to undertake part-time study, you may be able to continue claiming Jobseeker's Allowance as long as you are still available for, and actively seeking work. What is meant by 'part-time study' will be in your individual Jobseeker's Agreement. As a part-time student, you may also be eligible for Housing/Council Tax Benefit in certain circumstances.

Please seek expert advice from the agencies mentioned above. Information on different types of benefits is on: www.dwp.gov.uk Regulations differ slightly in Scotland and Northern Ireland.

Trade unions

Trade unions have always been involved in providing education and training for their members. If you are a member of a trade union, you may be entitled to financial help (although there are limiting criteria) through the General Federation of Trade Unions Education Trust. In addition, the Union Learning Fund supports various union learning projects, from the provision of basic skills courses right through to establishing workplace learning centres. There are networks of union learner representatives and lifelong learning advisers can give you information.

Employers

Don't forget that employers have always been a significant sponsor of education and training. As direct government support for students is squeezed, they may be expected to share more of the burden. Some employers have achieved the Investors in People award which shows that it should take the development of its staff seriously. Some employers run their own employee development programmes. Many postgraduate masters programmes rely heavily on commercial sponsorship. In fact, without employers paying fees and other expenses, many people wouldn't be able to afford to study. Whatever course you plan to take, if you are in employment, you should regard your employer as a potential source of assistance. It is always worth approaching your employer about assistance and/or time off for study.

Part-time work

Many students – including those on full-time, higher-education courses – subsidise their education and training through working at weekends, in the evenings or on tuition-free days. Universities and colleges often help students to find suitable part-time work with local firms; some even offer bar work, cleaning jobs, basic clerical work etc on-campus to students. Any work experience – especially for those who have not been in a work situation for some time – may help to improve the skills of teamwork, communication, problem solving or ICT, however irrelevant the job may seem to your future career.

Learning overseas

There are a number of books and websites with information about funding for education and training overseas. The Socrates-Erasmus programme funds higher-education students who choose to spend part of their course in another European Union country. The Leonardo programme encourages vocational training throughout Europe.

If you are interested in learning overseas (in the EU, a Commonwealth country or elsewhere in the world), some useful contacts are given below.

UK Socrates-Erasmus Council – Research and Development Building, The University, Canterbury CT2 7PD. Tel: 01227 762712. Annually publishes *Experience Erasmus: The UK Guide* in association with ISCO Publications (tel: 01276 21188), £14.95. www.erasmus.ac.uk

Information on **Leonardo** can be found on: www.leonardo.org.uk

The Fulbright Commission – US Educational Advisory Service – Fulbright House, 62 Doughty Street, London WC1N 2JZ. Tel: 020 7404 6994. Contact for information on funding for study in the US. www.fulbright.co.uk

Association of Commonwealth Universities – John Foster House, 36 Gordon Square, London WC1H 0PF. Tel: 020 7380 6700. www.acu.ac.uk

For a guide to higher-education opportunities in Europe: www.eurochoice.org.uk

Study Abroad – published by UNESCO. 2004-05 edition, £17.50. Available from The Stationery Office, tel: 0870 600 5522

Exodus – a database of international careers information produced by Careers Europe.

Further information

Throughout this chapter, sources of information and advice have been given for each topic. More general sources of information and advice are given below.

As a starting point for information and advice about funding your learning, you can contact your:

- **local adult information, advice and guidance agency**

- **learning provider** – colleges, universities etc are increasingly concerned about the financial plight of students so offer advice and guidance e.g. through student support offices, welfare centres or even student financial advice centres

- **students' union** (N.B. information sheets on student finance can be downloaded from the website of the National Union of Students – choose 'money' from the 'advice' menu and then click on 'information sheets library': www.nusonline.co.uk)

- **Citizens Advice Bureaux** – staff are able to provide guidance on the benefits system and on dealing with financial problems. Offices will have information about sources of funding, including any local initiatives. They will also be able to refer you to other agencies. The service is free and confidential. Information is also on: www.adviceguide.org.uk

Possible sources of information, advice and support in the different parts of the UK include:

- local **Learning and Skills Councils** (which are responsible for funding further education and training for those over 16 in **England**)

- the **Scottish Executive Enterprise and Lifelong Learning Department** which is responsible for further and higher education, skills and lifelong learning in Scotland; funding is administered through the **Students Award Agency for Scotland**

- the **National Council for Education and Training in Wales** and the **Higher Education Funding Council for Wales** which are responsible for all post-16 education and training

- the **Department for Employment and Learning in Northern Ireland** which is responsible for further and higher education and training; funding is administered by the local **Education and Library Boards**.

Useful websites include:

- www.waytolearn.co.uk (has information on financing adult learning)

- www.studentmoney.org (provides information on planning and organising your finances)

- learndirect: www.learndirect.co.uk (advice line: 0800 100 900)

- learndirect Scotland: www.learndirectscotland.com (advice line: 0808 100 9000).

Chapter six
Making your choice

So far this book has considered many aspects of learning, and provided information about the qualifications, possible providers, costs and so on. Sooner or later, the time comes when you have to make a decision about whether to embark on learning, and which opportunity to opt for.

In order to make a choice, you need to:

- be clear about what you are aiming to achieve

- identify all the relevant opportunities

- find out as much as you can about them

- then weigh up the pros and cons of each!

Work out your aims

Possible reasons for returning to learning could include:

- to pursue an interest

- for self-development

- to improve your careers prospects

- to improve your qualifications

- to help your kids with their homework

- to improve your confidence

- just for the fun of it

– or, perhaps a combination of all of these! Even though you may not have worked out your long-term aims in detail, you should at least have a broad idea of your reasons for embarking on learning, and what you hope to achieve in the short term.

If your reasons for considering a return to learning relate to your future work plans, you will, of course, need to decide on a career avenue – this might not be a specific job, but you will need a broad career area in mind. Plenty of information about the qualification requirements of particular occupations can be found in reference books, on websites, databases and other careers resources, held in your local adult information, advice and guidance agency. If you find yourself going round in circles when considering future career plans, these agencies can help.

> *'My reason for returning to college was to gain the qualification I needed to carry on my long-term career prospects.'*

Take one step at a time

You do not need to start out with a complete plan. Not everybody returning to learning has a clear idea about what they want to achieve ultimately, and most would admit to having doubts about what they are capable of achieving. People often underestimate their own abilities, and many end up studying at a level way above their initial expectations. But, once started, you also find that your ideas change, new interests develop and, as you gain confidence, you often find that one programme or course leads naturally to another.

The most important thing is to decide on your starting point.

> *'As the old Chinese saying goes " a one mile or one hundred mile journey starts with one step".'*

Build on your previous experience

As an adult learner, you don't need to start at the bottom each time. You have two assets over school-leavers: maturity and experience. And, through working – even through living – you acquire skills and knowledge over and above those acquired through education. It is important to take these as your starting points.

Advisers in education and training organisations recognise that adults bring additional qualities and are not starting straight from school. As described in chapter three, through the process of APL, APEL etc, recognition for skills/knowledge you have learned outside a formal educational or training environment, as well as those acquired on other courses can sometimes be gained. Many admissions tutors are prepared to waive standard entry requirements if you have relevant work experience, though you may be asked to sit an aptitude test or take a preparatory course.

Identify all the relevant opportunities

Making good decisions requires having all the relevant information. In this respect, there is no substitute for getting detailed information from learning providers. But, course programmes and college prospectuses can only tell part of the story; these can seem daunting, presenting you with a complex selection of choices and options. So how do you find out what courses are really like?

There are two practical steps you can take.

- The **first step** is to talk to people who have first-hand experience, not just course tutors and admissions officers, but also current and former students.

- The **second step** is to try something out. Whatever your aims in returning to learning – whether recreational, vocational or academic – there are ways of easing yourself in gently. Enrol on a short course in a subject that interests you or take one of the 'return to study' courses which are designed to help you explore your options.

In chapter nine, sources of information and advice are discussed in detail. In summary, to find out where particular courses are available:

- contact local **information, advice and guidance agencies** for adults

- consult local and national **databases** of courses which may be available for you to use in the above agencies, or in libraries and at the Jobcentre Plus/Jobcentre

- consult **learndirect** – the national helpline for information about courses, tel: 0800 100 900 (www.learndirect.co.uk) or in Scotland on 0808 100 9000 (www.learndirectscotland.com)

- get hold of the **prospectuses** of all local colleges, or colleges within travelling range of your home. If you are considering distance learning, identify possible providers (see chapter four) and get hold of brochures.

Find out as much as you can about each opportunity

Seek to answer the following.

- Where does the course lead?

- What does the course content cover?

- How is the course structured and delivered – does that fit into your lifestyle?

- What about the learning provider – its reputation, facilities and support services?

- What about the cost – put simply, can you afford it?

Let's consider these five questions in more detail.

Where does the course lead?

You may need to consider how useful any certificate or award will be both in terms of openings into careers and jobs and in terms of entry to further professional study or higher education. You need to balance the merits of gaining a general award like an economics A level, for example, against a specific qualification for a particular trade or occupation.

Some key questions

- Is the award widely recognised by employers?

- Is the qualification necessary to achieve a higher position at work or within your profession?

- Is it a recognised entry qualification for higher-level academic courses?

- Are you clear about which higher-level courses you could progress onto?

- Will the qualification help you to achieve your long-term goals; for example, is it necessary for the career change you wish to make?

What does the course content cover?

- You need to get beyond course titles and find out what the course actually covers. For example, even degrees in seemingly straightforward subjects, such as history and mathematics, vary considerably between institutions. It's important to study something that sustains your interest, so make sure you are aware of the topics covered.

- Will you have to make decisions about options within the course?

- Are you ready for the demands of the course – or do you need to do some preparatory study first?

- How is the course assessed? Is that in a manner that suits you?

- What are the entry requirements, if any? Are you, as an adult applicant, expected to meet them, or can they be relaxed in view of other experience and qualifications that you can offer?

  'My advice to those returning to study is to choose your subject well, enthusiasm really enhances your chances of success.'

How is the course structured and delivered?

A more practical consideration, but one of equal importance, will concern the way the course is organised and structured. This will have a large bearing on whether it can be successfully combined with your current work and domestic responsibilities.

Find a course that suits your personal circumstances

The most common reason why adults drop out of learning is because they are over-committed. When you have conflicting domestic and work responsibilities, study can take a back seat.

Time pressures, more than anything else, can lead to discouragement and disillusionment. Take advantage of the flexibility offered by colleges and other providers to find a course that complements, rather than clashes with, your other responsibilities. You can always switch to more intensive or full-time courses as you become more confident and committed.

Coping with the additional domestic and social pressures that a return to learning can bring is looked at more fully in the next chapter.

Course structure and delivery – the key questions

- How is the course delivered – is it full-time, part-time or through open or distance learning?

- How much independent study time is required outside the timetabled classroom/learning sessions? How realistic is that for you?

- How much flexibility does the course structure offer you? Should you need to take a break from the course, will that present problems? Or is the course structured on a modular or unit basis, which you build up as you go along?

- Will you be assigned a personal tutor? What kind and level of support will he/she provide?

Richard Haines – found a flexible way to learn

Richard, 49 from Kensington, was a self-employed gardener until three years ago when a slipped disc forced him to rethink his career. He then enrolled on a learndirect introduction to computers course, and later progressed to courses in desktop publishing, computer art and computer animation.

'I knew if I was going to get back into the job market I'd need to know how to use a computer. I was completely computer illiterate – I didn't even know how to hold a mouse – and I found the prospect of starting from scratch rather daunting. I was nervous about having to keep up with other people, so the flexibility of learndirect really appealed to me. The option of being able to work at my own pace and the encouraging and friendly staff at the library soon overcame my hesitation.

learndirect is a great way for people to get started in using computers, and the library is peaceful and comfortable. I did four learndirect courses there, including office skills and website design, and even joined two group classes.

Rather than just seeing computers as something I needed to know about in order to find work, I started to realise that I'd like to work with computers. I was completely unaware of their graphic design possibilities, and I'm now really interested in that side of things. It's unbelievable what you can do with the right software.

Developing computer skills has enhanced both my job prospects and my creativity. I can't draw to save my life, and it's very satisfying to be able to produce beautiful pictures with the computer.

I'm now doing a video production course. Half the time is spent out filming, and the other half is editing on the computer. The course ends in a work-experience placement and an industry-recognised qualification, and I'm hoping to find work as a film editor. It's amazing to think I've gone from being a complete technophobe to a computer graphics enthusiast!'

What about the learning provider?

A wide range of organisations offer learning opportunities, so it's wise to find out as much as you can about the provider, and the facilities and services they offer.

- Has the provider a good **reputation**? Do you have contacts who have been on other courses at the same institution – or even better, on the same course as you are considering? Be careful not to put too much weight on one person's opinion, but if you hear certain criticisms repeatedly, you may want to check those aspects out particularly carefully. For example, if people comment on the lack of access to ICT facilities, or the time it takes to get work marked and returned, you may choose to ask pertinent questions of admissions staff about such aspects.

- Does the learning provider make **adult learners welcome**?

- What about **learner support**? For instance, is there extra help with study skills, or support with English and maths?

- Is there an effective **student welfare** service?

- What are the **library** facilities like? Are there sufficient copies of essential texts etc?

- Are the **ICT facilities** sufficient for your needs, e.g. for wordprocessing or conducting research?

- **Childcare** provision – is it available? Are there places available? Where is it sited in relation to your course base?

- **Transport/parking** for students – find out if there are good public transport links. Are there car parks? If so, will space be available when you need it?

These are all aspects of learning that are easily overlooked when considering choice of learning or provider, but they could make a crucial difference to your success. Some of these aspects, including childcare provision and support services, are discussed in more depth in the next chapter.

> *'Make use of the help you can receive from your colleagues, tutors, friends and family. You can always return a favour at a later date.'*

What about course costs?

This is the big question! As described in the last chapter, student funding is a complex area. Make sure that you have a realistic idea of the total cost involved, especially if you could not otherwise afford to start the course. As emphasised in chapter five, ask about all the 'hidden' costs, such as for books, materials, examination entry fees, or even visits and fieldtrips. And don't forget to take into account your travel costs etc!

However, remember that financial support is available for many students, and, of course, if you are on a government-funded programme, your learning is free.

Weighing up the pros and cons

So, you have identified your options, found out all you possibly can about each, looked into the finances and considered all the practicalities.

Ideally, you will be left with a shortlist of one course, which meets all your needs! However, life being as it is, it's more likely that you will have narrowed down to a few learning opportunities, each of which has various pros and cons, possibly leaving you still uncertain as to the best option.

Firstly, make sure that you have got **all** the information you need. If you still have unanswered questions that prevent you from being able to come to a decision, contact the learning provider and ask.

One approach to decision making is simply to write down a list of pros and cons for each opportunity. Try to be as specific as you can about each advantage and disadvantage. This process can, in itself, help to crystallise your thoughts. Just seeing the pros and cons written in black and white can help.

Look in particular at the disadvantages you have identified. How great are these? Are they all **really** drawbacks? Perhaps some can be overcome. For example, if costs are one of your concerns, are you sure there is no available financial assistance, or ways of paying, that could help? If you are concerned that you may not cope with the written assignments, perhaps there is study skills support that you are not aware of? Always remember there may be 'ways round' perceived problems. Contact the admissions tutor and talk over your concerns with him or her.

Remember, it is always useful to talk over decisions with someone else, preferably someone that is impartial, independent and who has some expertise. Staff based in adult information, advice and guidance agencies can help you to assess the best learning option for you. Do make use of their services.

'Learning has given me a new focus, a new structure to my life and set of aims and objectives that I feel I am well on the way to achieving.'

Further information

Some, or all, of the resources listed below should be available in your local adult information, advice and guidance agency. In addition, agencies usually have databases of occupations and learning opportunities that you can consult.

Agencies may also have a computerised career-guidance system that you can use. An example is *Adult Directions* which generates job suggestions based on your likes and dislikes.

Build Your Own Rainbow – a workbook for career and life management, available from Trotman, £15.00.

Test Your Own Aptitude – published by Kogan Page, £8.99.

Keynotes – from Lifetime Careers Publishing. A series of learning/career guidance leaflets for adults. (N.B. *Keynotes Plus!* is the computerised version of Keynotes.)

Second Chances – A national guide to adult education and training opportunities – published by Lifetime Careers Publishing.

Chapter seven
Taking the plunge

'The opportunity to learn new skills and improve my standard of education was what I was looking for, and to achieve this, I would have to gain qualifications. I decided to take the plunge and return to learning to allow me to fulfil this goal.'

The words of one happy returner!

The previous chapters of this book have taken you through the different ways you can learn and the various qualifications you can gain. Hopefully, the book has also answered a few questions or addressed problems about finance. If you've made some choices, based on this information, it's time to consider taking the plunge.

Perhaps the biggest barrier preventing more adults from studying is psychological. Returning to learning represents a step into the unknown. It generates concerns about doing coursework, writing essays and taking exams. If you have been away from full-time education for some years, it is easy to question your own abilities or to fear failure. And there is some understandable unease about placing yourself in new situations and environments.

Preparing for your return

These concerns can be summarised in a single question: will I be able to cope? The answer, as the individual stories throughout this book illustrate, is that, with good planning and guidance at the outset, most people manage extremely successfully. The main thing is to make sure that you are likely to enjoy the subject you study. You will need to keep motivated for several years of study, and pressures you may face during the course are not always obvious at the beginning of your studies.

Sandra Small – training to get back into the classroom!

Sandra decided to do a PGCE course after several years as a classroom assistant. She has some helpful advice for those about to 'take the plunge'.

'For many years I had been interested in primary teaching, but always dismissed it as impossible; after all, raising three children didn't exactly leave a great deal of time to indulge in pursuing my own career! As a result, the idea remained firmly on the back burner and remained just that – an idea. For many years I contented myself with helping out at my son's primary school as a classroom assistant and serving as a governor, all of which turned out to be invaluable experience. As soon as I felt the time was right for my family, I applied for training. To my surprise, I was called for an interview to the University of the West of England, in Bristol. The interview was very relaxed and informal, and I found that my 'work experience' stood me in good stead. I was offered a place on the PGCE course.

The first day at Bristol was nerve racking, and I felt very old, but I quickly realised that I wasn't the only one who was nervous. There was an interesting mix of ages and life experiences; for example, a fellow student began the course having recently had her second child, whereas others had returned from a year out after taking their first degree. We were allocated to a tutor group of about 20 students and worked mainly within that group. The group began to 'gel' surprisingly quickly, perhaps due to the intensity of the course; we supported and learned from each other. The course was completely different to a degree course, being vocational – we were told at the outset to expect a 9 to 5 day at least, with very little free time as there was so much to cram into one year.

The run-up to Christmas was particularly hectic for those of us with family responsibilities; we definitely felt the extra pressure! I found the travelling exhausting, and the volume of work soul-destroying at times – I still remember forcing myself

---

to stay awake on the train to finish some prescribed reading! However, the feeling of achievement on completing the course was unforgettable, like winning a gold medal! Looking back, I think the support and understanding of my family was crucial; the whole venture would have been impossible without that – unless you happen to be Wonder Woman! To any would-be mature students out there, I would recommend the following points as a means of staying sane:

- *if you have family responsibilities, make sure everyone is supportive and realises the need to help out*

- *outline how they can help if you need to!*

- *be organised and prioritise – you can't do it all at once! Set yourself realistic, achievable targets*

- *allocate a bit of time each week just for you so that you can relax and escape for a while – go to the gym, see a film or just soak in the bath! It's amazing how it recharges the batteries, and you produce better work as a result.*

Don't be afraid to ask for help if you need to – it keeps problems in perspective.

Lastly, enjoy being a student – good luck!'

As Sandra says, coming back to learning can be challenging. This chapter looks at some of the problems adults face and the ways that these can be tackled. It is organised into two parts:

- study skills

- domestic and social pressures.

The first half, on study skills, covers essay and examination phobia, describes ways of preparing for study and looks at the support available to those at university and college. The second half of this chapter deals with some of the domestic and social pressures of returning to learning. It examines how to make the time to study, and tackles issues such as how to combine learning with looking after children and dependants.

Most importantly, it tells you that you do not have to manage everything on your own. There is a variety of support available to help you overcome problems. Increasingly, colleges are putting extra emphasis on 'learner support services', which are designed both to help students learn more effectively and to care for their welfare.

Study skills

Mature students sometimes have a reflex inferiority complex. They feel that their work is not up to standard, that they will not be able to write essays, and that they will fail exams. If your previous experience of education at school was not very positive, or if you were not very successful, then these fears can seem more like home truths than mere conjectures. However, in general:

- older students tend to do better than those that join university straight from school or sixth-form college

- those that enter university without traditional qualifications can do as well as those admitted with the standard two or three A levels – good A level results are no guarantee of success in university

- mature students consistently achieve higher degree classification.

There have been few similar studies in further education, but the anecdotal evidence suggests the same: mature students do well. Older students are generally welcome in further and higher education because they work harder, are well motivated, have already developed time management skills and, with their valuable experience, they contribute more to courses. It should be reassuring to know that adults returning to education tend to do well. But how do you know whether you will cope? How can you improve your study skills? There are several practical steps you can take by:

- preparing for study
- confronting essay and exam phobia
- using learner support services
- building confidence.

Study preparation

There are many courses which are specifically designed to help adults prepare for a return to study. Courses with titles such as 'return to study' or 'second chance to learn' prepare you for longer programmes in further and higher education. Access courses are designed for adults who wish to take degrees and other higher education qualifications but lack the formal entry requirements. They aim to provide the knowledge and skills needed to do a degree or diploma. All these courses include a specific element devoted to helping you learn effectively. Typically, this will include practical advice on:

- study skills

- use of learning resources

- examination techniques.

But, importantly, these programmes also offer a more gradual return to education. They are an opportunity to test the water, to assess your options and, crucially, to build some confidence in your own abilities. So, if you are lacking confidence, an Access course may be beneficial even if you have the qualifications to be accepted immediately onto a degree course. Some Access courses are specifically tailored towards particular courses or disciplines, such as Access to nursing or humanities. The QAA (Qualifications Assurance Agency) recognises more than 1000 Access programmes.

An alternative way of preparing for study is to take a distance learning course. For example, the National Extension College runs 'getting started' courses on study skills with titles such as 'How to write essays', and 'How to study effectively'. The Open University has several useful study packs. These include a huge range of short courses (at level one) designed to get people back into the swing of studying before starting a longer course. The Openings programme of short introductory courses gives you the chance to:

- work on your study skills

- build up your confidence

- get a taste of your chosen subject

- decide what you want to study in the future.

All new OU students are sent a preparatory package before the start of a course to help them brush up their skills. Finally, there is the do-it-yourself approach. You can prepare for a course by background reading, using self-study materials and even by doing practice essays. If you have been accepted onto a course, then ask tutors what would be the most useful preparation to undertake to help bring you up to speed.

Essay and exam phobia

Education often conjures up visions of essays and examinations. When leaving school or college for the last time, many people experience relief from knowing that it is finally over. Understandably, the thought of going through it all again can be a major barrier to returning to study. So, how do you overcome the fear of essays and exams?

The most important thing to do is to put the problem into perspective. Essays can seem difficult but often the difficulties are not due to lack of ability. One of the most common problems arises from the fact that adults set themselves high standards; they want to do well and judge themselves harshly. They fear failure and 'loss of face'. Consequently, if you think that everything you write is not good enough, it becomes very difficult to write anything.

Exams can seem daunting because they are often seen as being the only determining factor in the final result. In recent years, however, there have been many changes in the way that courses are assessed. There has been a move away from complete reliance on traditional examinations. Both in further and higher education, there is more use of continuous assessment and assignment-based assessment. In vocational education, the trend is towards competence-based courses; you are judged on your performance in real situations, rather than your ability to pass theoretical exams.

Like any phobia, the way to deal with worries about essays or exams is to confront them head-on. The key is practice: the more you do, the easier it becomes. If you are out of practice – unlike school-leavers, most adults will have taken a lengthy break from education – there are some practical steps you can take. There are two main options. First, you can undertake some preparatory study, before starting a longer course, which will help you build up confidence and develop study skills. Courses like those mentioned in the study preparation section above should help with essay writing and exams. Second, you can take advantage of the support offered by many colleges and universities through learning resource centres and similar facilities.

The BBC, through its adult learner programme, runs a selection of online courses including Skillswise, which provides factsheets, exercises and games designed to help with English and maths. There are also a variety of online courses in health, computers and IT, languages, history and gardening. Have a look at www.bbc.co.uk/learning/adults

Learner support services

Learner support services is a widely-used term for the measures that many colleges and universities are introducing to help their students learn effectively. These services are increasingly common, not least because of demand created by the numbers of people returning to education after several years away from studying. But the measures are also designed to support new ways of teaching, which place less emphasis on lectures and seminars and provide more opportunities for supported private study and group work with other students.

Help with study skills comes in several guises. The skills covered will typically include note-taking, writing, revision methods and exam techniques. In some courses, it is an integral part of the learning programme. Many colleges and universities have set up study skills centres or provide other resources which students can use on an occasional basis when they have a specific problem. Others rely on advice through more informal contacts with personal tutors.

Many colleges pay particular attention to people with disabilities or with specific learning difficulties. This includes help for those who have visual or hearing impairments and those who have conditions such as dyslexia that can affect studying. In addition, many have tutors to help improve basic numeracy and literacy skills, as well as offering a range of English language teaching for speakers of other languages.

If you do find coping with the coursework or exams difficult (and everybody has problems at some stage), then there are sources of help and advice; you can approach tutors, fellow students or staff in learning resources centres. You **do not** have to work through every problem by yourself.

Confidence

Confidence, or the lack of it, plays a big role in returning to learning. You may feel that everyone will be younger than you or that you will be out-of-touch with the learning process. Many older students expect to be 'found out', feeling that they are not up to the academic demands. It rarely happens. Few mature students drop out simply because they cannot cope with the academic work, although many have doubts at the start – the younger students are brighter, the college made a mistake in admitting me, my coursework isn't up to standard.

The main point to emphasise is that this passes. Worries are usually more to do with confidence and self-belief than academic ability. You gain confidence from completing assignments successfully. But you also gain confidence from other places and people. Fellow students are often extremely helpful, and working together can help to build confidence, as well as creating the opportunity to make new friends.

'I have gained many things from my learning experience not just the qualifications I have obtained and hope to gain at college but also the improvement of my self-confidence.'

Tutors and lecturers are generally supportive. They do not tend to

Dermot Moorehead – proving you're never too old!

Dermot's stroke convinced him to take the plunge and return to college after 50 years in the workplace. He studied for a GCSE in English.

'Three years ago I had a massive stroke at the age of 63. I went from being a very fit person, swimming a mile a night after work, to what I would call a

vegetable. Doctors and welfare said that returning to learning would keep my mind active, as sitting all day doing nothing was not good for me. So on leaving hospital I entered into further education.

I found it very difficult to push myself to start college, as I left school with no qualifications over fifty years ago – the thought of starting again was daunting. I had to motivate myself, but in the end the pleasure outweighed the difficulties, as all the tutors and staff were marvellous and they always give one hundred and ten percent to me and all the students.

At the age of 66 I had not planned to return to study to benefit my career – I had already been forced to retire as a result of my stroke. But I have to say much to my surprise that I enjoyed the experience of going back to college, possibly because I had nothing to lose and everything to gain. I told the rest of the class "I was here only for the fun", as most of them were the same age as my granddaughter! A lot of the young ones needed the high grades for their career and future, but I really enjoyed their company.

The hardest part of going back to school is enrolling on the first day, when you look around the class you see that the ages range from sixteen to seventy. But if you look at their faces they seem more scared than you feel! I set myself a goal to attend every class and not worry about learning, but as the classes roll on the learning clicks into automatic pilot. If I learned one new thing I would count that as a bonus. As the old Chinese saying goes "a one mile or one hundred mile journey starts with one step". The hardest part of the journey is leaving the house, as you are trying to find any excuse not to go to the class. Once you have closed your front door you are three quarters of the way there, and you will enjoy it.'

patronise or talk down to adults; as mentioned above, many actively welcome the contribution and enthusiasm that older people bring to the classroom. But equally, they are aware that adults have uncertainties about returning to education, so they try to offer encouragement to help people build up self-confidence. Nonetheless, in the final analysis, choosing to return to study is up to you. Most people surprise themselves with what they can do. You may start with anxieties and doubts, but you will end with a sense of achievement.

*'It has helped improve my self-esteem, and taught me to pay **no** attention to discouragement and disillusionment from within or without. It has also made me realise that with the right ingredients, the sky **is** indeed the limit.'*

Domestic and social pressures

Education offers the possibility of change. For many mature students it provides a big stimulus and lift, but for their partners it may be threatening or stressful. They can feel that they are being left behind or missing out. It is perhaps understandable that relationships can suffer; indeed, some fail. But there are other, perhaps more mundane, pressures that arise from the effort of trying to do too much. Not only do most mature students have to run a home and earn a living, but also keep up family commitments as well as finding time to study. Choosing to study is by no means an easy option.

As a result, though mature students rarely drop out of courses because of lack of ability or lack of money, some find that it becomes difficult to cope with the effect that studying has with regard to family and partners. Studying need not be stressful or pressurised, but you need to be able to face up to the demands it generates. Before the course, you should be aware of some of the potential problems and pitfalls.

Key questions to ask yourself

- Can you find/make the time needed each week not only to attend classes, but also to study and complete assignments?

- Will you be able to combine studying with caring for children and dependant relatives?

- Will partners feel excluded or neglected?

- Do you need to spend nights or weeks away from home?

- Is travel to and from college convenient or manageable?

It may not be possible to answer all these questions satisfactorily before you start out. Some problems will only materialise during the course.

But there are ways of anticipating problems and establishing support systems. You can make things easier for yourself by enlisting the help of friends and relatives. You can also benefit from the increasing amount of support available from colleges and universities. Some provide practical help with childcare, a few offer assistance with transport and most run some kind of welfare service.

'Guilt will be a factor to consider, as you may sometimes feel that the family is being left out, or the housework is not being done. Sometimes there are also worries about being able to keep up to date with the work, which can be stressful and lead to the occasional sleepless night.'

Support systems

Perhaps the most obvious way of minimising pressure is to plan your education wisely. Be aware of the time, money and effort required, and be careful not to take on too much. This is not written to put you off studying, rather to suggest that you need to find the right course at the right time. And you need the support systems to help you manage.

For example, if you are bringing up children then there are a number of issues to weigh up in deciding when to return to learning. When children are pre-school age, studying is difficult unless there is affordable nursery provision. Even when children are at school, full-time education might be impractical unless you can arrange after-school and holiday care. You need to think about finding the time to study; with young children you have the evenings free, as they grow older you might need to negotiate free time with your partner.

If you are working, you need to weigh the effect on your career of any study breaks. You might want to avoid taking on an extra activity during periods when your job is particularly demanding. You need to balance the effects of any possible loss of income against future benefits. Whatever decision you make, you are more likely to make a success of education if you receive support from others. This can come from several sources.

Family

If you are married or in a long-term relationship, it is important to have the support and backing of your partner. You may also need practical support such as an agreement to look after the kids at the weekend so that you have peace and quiet to study.

Friends

In returning to learning, you may sometimes feel that you have to prove something, not just to yourself but also to friends and colleagues. Ideally, friends should be on your side and a source of encouragement, but if they are disparaging, use it as a source of strength and resolve to prove them wrong.

Fellow students

Education can be isolating if you are studying at home alone, and just attending college for classes. Find time to socialise with fellow students, reassure yourself that other people are having to deal with the same kinds of problems as you. Some universities have mature students' societies that organise social activities and act as an informal support system for older students.

> *'If you are a mature student like me, you will experience the joy of learning new things and the comradeship of a group of people helping and supporting one another.'*

Employer

If you are working, your employer may be prepared to help you organise your time better so that there is room for study. Some employers will grant flexible hours or a temporary switch to part-time working, others allow (unpaid) sabbaticals and study leave.

Childcare

Education providers recognise that many adults, especially women, are effectively prevented from returning to education unless they can find adequate nursery and crèche facilities for their children while they attend classes. Many courses aimed at women, such as programmes for those wishing to return to work or daytime adult education classes, simply would not attract sufficient numbers to be viable unless free or cheap childcare were made available.

University and college nurseries

An increasing number of universities and colleges have nurseries to look after the children of both staff and students. Places are often extremely limited, so you should apply as soon as possible. Contact the Student Services office of your chosen HE institution to find out what's available and how much it will cost. Policy on nursery fees varies enormously; some colleges heavily subsidise the service, others set fees to recoup their costs.

Even if they have very few facilities themselves, colleges and universities may be able to provide useful information on local childcare facilities.

Looking after school-age children

Colleges are aware that parental responsibilities do not end when children start attending school. Some have introduced more flexibility into their timetables, making it easier for parents to take classes in the middle of the day, so leaving them the time to take and fetch children to and from school. Some run programmes that coincide with school terms, taking breaks during holidays and half-term. However, many courses still overlap with school holidays or have classes scheduled outside school hours. Although some colleges and universities now run schemes for school-age children, in practice most parents will have to make their own arrangements for their children after school and during holidays.

Other sources of help

If you have to make your own arrangements for your children while you are attending classes, then your options include helpful friends and relatives, childminders, state nurseries, private nurseries and play centres, and after-school play schemes. The Government's National Childcare Strategy is designed to help overcome the problems of childcare while you are learning. At present, there are free childcare places for three-

and four- year-olds in early years education: some in private and state nurseries but, increasingly, primary schools are creating their own nursery units to accommodate them. In the latest Government spending review, plans were unveiled to extend free nursery provision to 12,000 two-year-olds in the most disadvantaged areas of the country by 2008.

To get a fuller picture of your options, you should explore all avenues of financial support and practical advice. Chapter five gives details of some of the grants available to help learners with children. Other relevant useful organisations are listed below.

learndirect helpline 0800 100 900 (0808 100 9000 for those in Scotland) can advise on childcare provision for people returning to learning and information is also available from www.learndirect-advice.co.uk or www.learndirectscotland.com

Gingerbread is a network of self-help support groups for single parents. Local groups may be contacted through the national office. Tel: 020 7488 9300. Advice line: 0800 018 4318. www.gingerbread.org.uk

Childcare Link 0800 096 0296 — 8am to 8pm Monday — Friday; 9am to midday on Saturday. A national freephone helpline to provide details of local Children's Information Service centres as well as childcare options in your area. www.childcarelink.gov.uk

Daycare Trust — Shoreditch Town Hall Annexe, 380 Old Street, London EC1V 9LT. Tel: 020 7739 2866. Can advise parents and employers on the quality and accessibility of childcare. www.daycaretrust.org.uk

Transport

The provision, time and cost of travel can cause persistent hassle to those returning to learning. Long and frequent journeys backwards and forwards to college don't just cost money; they eat up time and they can be tiring.

There are only a limited number of ways in which you can restrict travel demands. The most obvious is to attend a college or education provider that is conveniently located. Unfortunately this may not be practicable:

local colleges may not be particularly accessible, or they may not run the courses you wish to take. If you have a difficult journey, you could try to organise a lift arrangement with fellow students. Ask if classes, tutorials and workshops can be arranged to minimise the number of journeys you have to make each week.

In general, education providers do realise that travel difficulties can restrict access to studying. Within their financial constraints, some try to offer support with transport.

Welfare services

Under the broad banner of student services, colleges and universities provide a range of practical help for students who have problems or are troubled in some way. This has two main strands, one concerned with effective learning (see learner support services above), the other with health, finance and welfare problems.

Although older students are often the last to admit that they have problems, it is useful to know that such help exists. If you do have a problem that is affecting your coursework, or if your course is having an adverse effect on the rest of your life, then there are people who can provide advice and support.

The specific services vary from institution to institution. However, most provide some of the following:

- confidential counselling

- advice on welfare rights and welfare benefits

- information on matters of finance

- educational guidance and careers advice

- assistance with childcare

- health care and/or health education.

Colleges organise this welfare service in various ways and under a number of names, including a student advisory and counselling service, or a counselling and support service. Some institutions link counselling services with educational and careers guidance, others with financial and grants advice.

You should note that welfare services can sometimes be very stretched. This means that you may have to wait some time for an appointment with a counsellor. However, most services dispense general information and advice to anyone who drops by. Students' unions are another source of help; many have a welfare office.

Applying for a course

If, having noted all the points raised in this chapter, you are ready to 'take the plunge', the next step is to apply for the course of your choice.

For places on most educational courses at colleges of further education, or those offered by independent providers

You should apply directly to the course provider. Recruitment for further education courses run at FE colleges is done directly by the colleges themselves.

Most colleges have streamlined application procedures through admissions and guidance units. The main enrolment period for courses is usually at the beginning of September. However, many colleges start postal or telephone enrolments in May or June, so courses can fill early. Some courses and flexible learning programmes recruit throughout the year and, in general, it is possible to join courses after the start of term providing they are not full. Admissions staff should be able to advise you about courses, flexible learning options, course costs and student facilities such as childcare.

Most applications to full-time higher education courses (degrees and HNDs) run at FE colleges are now done via UCAS.

For courses at degree and diploma of higher education level

Courses at universities and colleges fall into two categories.

Those for which you apply direct to the university or college running the course

If you wish to study on any part-time or short course, a distance learning course or on most postgraduate courses, you apply direct to the university or college. (Exceptions to this are postgraduate teacher-training courses and social work.)

Those for which you apply through a central admissions service

To study on a full-time (or sandwich) foundation degree, degree, diploma or Higher National Diploma (HND) course, or for postgraduate qualifications in teacher training or social work, you apply through a **central admissions service**. This processes applications to all institutions offering HE courses in the UK. Sometimes referred to as clearing houses, details of the separate admissions services are given below. Each service deals with a specific range of courses.

You can apply at any time, although you will stand more chance of acceptance if you make an early application. For full-time degree courses, for example, applicants are advised to apply between September and January in the year prior to entry. However, many universities are sympathetic to late applications from mature students.

In general, universities are happy to advise potential mature students on applications procedures. Before making an application through the central admissions system, it may be worth making a direct approach to a university initially, particularly if you are only able to study at your local institution. If you are in any doubt about where and how to apply for a particular course, then speak to the admissions office of the college or university running that course. Provide them with a detailed CV, and see if you can arrange an appointment.

The central admissions services are:

Universities and Colleges Admissions Service (UCAS). UCAS, Rosehill, New Barn Lane, Cheltenham GL52 3ZD. UCAS handles applications for almost all full-time and sandwich courses at universities and higher education colleges leading to the award of a degree, Diploma of Higher Education (DipHE) and Higher National Diploma (HND). Application materials can be ordered online or from 0870 1122211. Admissions are currently made via one of three options: paper, EAS or ucasapply.

ucasapply is a web-based system, likely to become the main mode of application by 2006. At present UCAS also operates an electronic application system (EAS) in schools and colleges, although 2005 will see the last applications made through EAS. For more information about applications see: www.ucas.ac.uk

Graduate Teacher Training Registry (GTTR). GTTR, Rosehill, New Barn Lane, Cheltenham GL52 3LZ. GTTR is the clearing house for Postgraduate Certificate in Education (PGCE) courses. Applications can be made online. www.gttr.ac.uk

Nursing and Midwifery Admissions Service (NMAS). NMAS, Rosehill, New Barn Lane, Cheltenham GL52 3LZ. Tel: 0870 1122206. NMAS handles applications for full-length, diploma-level, pre-registration nursing and midwifery diploma courses. Application packs can be ordered online. www.nmas.ac.uk

N.B. SWAS (Social Work Admissions System) ceased to exist as an application system from September 2004. Institutions recruit directly or through UCAS for courses which were previously in the SWAS scheme.

As a general rule, the earlier you apply for educational courses, the better your chances of acceptance. This is certainly true for very popular courses like the Open University's arts programmes. Do not wait for the 'right time' to make an application. You might find that you are pushing at an open door: there may be late cancellations or some places may be held for 'non-traditional' entrants.

For a Government-funded training place

For Work-based Learning for Adults (WBLA), Training for Work in Scotland – the training programme for unemployed adults from 25 and over – your starting point will normally be at the Jobcentre Plus/ Jobcentre. You normally need to have been out of work for more than six months. Your eligibility will need to be checked, and other necessary administration undertaken.

WBLA aims to give you the chance to train or experience the type of work that interests you. More information is available on the website. www.jobcentreplus.gov.uk

Further information

An A-Z of Exam Survival – published by Trotman, £9.99.

The Good Study Guide – published by the Open University, £9.99 is helpful in developing study skills for OU foundation courses.

How to Study – published by Kogan Page, £8.99.

Second Chances – is a DfES publication which may be available for reference in careers libraries. It can also be found on the website. www.second-chances.uk.com

Keynotes – a series of careers guidance leaflets for adults, published by Lifetime Careers Publishing. The series may be available for reference in careers libraries.

The *Prospects* website provides lots of case studies from adults returning to learning. www.prospects.ac.uk

To find details of all the further and higher education courses on offer, turn to chapter four for a list of course directories. These should be available for consultation in libraries and adult guidance agencies.

Chapter eight
Onwards and upwards

Returning to learning can be an extremely positive experience. All the profiles contributed to this book endorse the fact that learning something new can provide a welcome mental challenge, giving people something to aim for, while, at the same time, developing new interests. And, often, at the end of a course of study there can be a sense of anticlimax; almost inevitably, people ask themselves **'What next?'**

Considerations

This chapter suggests some ways of continuing with — and building on — your learning. It looks briefly at how you can weigh up and explore options in academic learning, vocational education and in employment. But, before that, it is worth underlining three points.

- You do **not** have to follow a plan. Not everything we do has to be for a particular goal or purpose. Studying is satisfying in its own right, and you can choose to do it for fun and general interest, when you have the time, the inclination and the opportunity.

- If, however, you do have a precise aim in mind, such as achieving further qualifications essential for your career, then it is worth doing careful planning at the outset, and monitoring your progress to make sure your plan remains valid and on track.

- Ideas change and develop over time. At every stage of your learning pathway, consult with people who can advise you on taking your next step. Sources of help and advice are listed at the end of this chapter and in chapter nine.

Many people – training providers, adult guidance advisers, human resource managers, student advisers, course tutors and directors of studies – can help you plan your next move. Keen to promote lifelong learning, all education providers appreciate the concept of progression in studies, and can offer people clear information on further courses, routes towards higher qualifications and vocational accreditation that can help you to find employment. Many people will not achieve their aims through a single course. Instead, there will be a longer (some would say lifelong) process of personal and career development.

Getting a taste for it

Adults often return to learning with some trepidation, unsure about their abilities. Typically, once they start, their confidence increases and they develop a taste for study.

So, for many people, a natural next step is to take another course, motivated either by a desire to push themselves further and explore new interests, or to gain higher and more useful qualifications. It is now much easier to progress from one course to another. One reason is that the majority of further and higher education programmes have flexible entry requirements for adult applicants. In some cases, completion of any previous course is taken as sufficient evidence of your ability to study. Credit transfer schemes may make it possible to use accreditation from your current course to gain acceptance onto further programmes. Also, depending on the course of study you have been following, it may be possible to gain exemption from parts of a new course (see the section on accreditation of prior learning or APL in chapter three).

Colleges and adult education centres have advisers who can help you to plan a further programme of study. Sometimes, this planning element is an integral part of the course. For example, return to learn courses are designed to help you assess your future options, and most people naturally progress from these programmes to other courses, whether with the same training or education provider, or another.

It is important to emphasise that there are no set pathways in the learning process. You will soon find that learning can lead in many directions, each with different outcomes. Even if your learning has been purely vocational you can make good use of the skills and attributes you have acquired in quite different settings.

> *'My only problem now is which choice to make, but, in a bit of an Educating Rita moment, I'll be the one making it...'*

Watersheds

There are several important points in the learning process where you need to make careful choices about your options. This does not apply so much to adult leisure and recreational studies, where the only significant decision is whether to take courses that lead to a recognised award or whether to continue with study for its own sake. These are not mutually incompatible, but there tends to be a distinction between courses which are assessed and those that are free from testing.

For most people, there is a need to weigh up the benefits and drawbacks of progressing to advanced-level or higher education, or – for those who have achieved a first degree – the possibility and desirability of taking your studies to postgraduate level.

Carole Dyer – mature postgrad

Carole's return to learning has led her to researching for a PhD while her daughter has been taking her A levels and her husband has been studying through the OU!

> *'Dental nursing was the reason I returned to learning. After leaving school, I joined the Royal Air Force. I'd planned to train as a nurse, but age restrictions meant another two years' wait, so I joined as a dental nurse with the possibility of*

re-mustering to nursing later. There, dental nursing seemed so thrilling, combined as it was with war-role training, the prospect of promotion, travel and, of course, men in uniform. Unfortunately my career ended with some rather archaic views on the role of women and the arrival of our daughter. My husband was still in the RAF and, because his occupation took precedence, I was left to build a 'career' from short-term, dead-end, mind-numbingly dull jobs of which dental nursing, quite different in civvy street, was the mainstay. Once my husband had left the RAF, an attempted resettlement in my native Yorkshire made me realise that it wasn't so much where I was doing the work, but what I was doing that was the cause of my discontent.

Whilst between jobs my husband suggested I "do something about it". I think he had a computing or secretarial course in mind and may well have chosen his words more carefully had he realised that, nine years on, I'd be researching an 80,000 word doctoral thesis. I soon found myself enrolled on an Access to Higher Education course, with the intention of becoming a primary school teacher, an idea that had developed over the previous couple of years. The fact that my O levels were unspectacular didn't count against me, and all the things I felt were just something that I'd done because I had to — holding down a job whilst bringing up a child with my husband away in the forces, etc — turned out to be very creditable 'life skills'. The Access course was something of a revelation. I had intended it to be a means to an end but I found other people, who also felt their education had been cut short and wanted to find something more fulfilling. Whilst juggling working, looking after family and home, and feeling guilty about time spent on assignments, we all found opinions, voices and even our brains, all while being eased back into learning by sympathetic tutors, an accommodating timetable and incredible camaraderie.

However, once at university, despite previous work experience, I soon realised that — notwithstanding the three hours a day travelling, not being able to work, being short of money, and family commitments — although I loved teaching the children, I didn't want to be mum and social worker to 28 seven-year-olds. Though I thoroughly enjoyed two of the subjects, history and English, I didn't really care for the others. When confronted with a boy who declared maths boring, it was a Herculean task not to agree with him. To be honest I found it tedious. So, when it came to the "are you the right person, in the right place, doing the right thing?" interview I answered no and became a university dropout.

I didn't know what to do next. Teaching still appealed, but until I'd decided I thought that a degree could only be useful, and as I'd found the history part of the previous courses so enjoyable, then that's what I would do. The following year I began a BA in history at a nearer university. The same problems regarding finances, travel, family, etc were as much in evidence, but at last I'd found something I really loved doing. Rather ironically, it was by working as a dental nurse that I funded my time there. By the end of year three, I'd decided to become a university lecturer, which thankfully involved continuing studying at PhD level. However, it had been five years since starting out and the intention was to do a course that would lead to employment. So, knowing I would still have to work whilst studying, I looked for a job. It took three years, two changes of profession and a house move before I, at last, began the PhD.

I have loved being back in education, although my current job is so boring. At each stage I've been provided with new experiences and opportunities. My only problem now is which choice to make, but, in a bit of an Educating Rita moment, I'll be the one making it, even if it is dental nursing. I've learned that having a degree doesn't make you a better person, nor an expert in everything. I still get road rage, can't get a computer to do anything – let alone what I want it to do – and yes, maths is still boring. But I do find myself, for the first time since leaving the RAF, perfectly content. Now if only I could find some lecturing work, funding for the PhD, someone to do the gardening…and my advice to anyone thinking of returning to learning – just do it.'

Key questions

If you are considering further study at the end of your present course, perhaps the best advice is to apply these five tests.

- Have I got the time?
- Can I afford it?
- Will I enjoy it?
- Would further study knit with or build on my previous qualifications?
- Will it improve my job prospects or benefit my career?

On to higher education?

Following advanced-level education – that is, courses which lead to qualifications at level 3, i.e. of a standard equivalent to A levels or BTEC National qualifications – the key decision is whether to progress to higher education.

Some people who gain level 3 qualifications go straight into – or remain in – employment, while many decide to progress to higher education – either full- or part-time. The majority of these study for degrees; others take a BTEC Higher National Diploma or Certificate (HND/HNC), a foundation degree or a Diploma in Higher Education (DipHE) course. The over-25s are the fastest-growing group of entrants to higher education, despite the difficulties of balancing their other commitments – financial and domestic – with studying. Of course, those who opt for employment at this stage can continue to make progress in their learning through work-based training and part-time study.

Higher and even higher?

For graduates, the choice is between:

* employment

* postgraduate education

* training.

Destination figures for 2002 graduates show that 18.7% continued with further study or training, while 66.9% found work in the UK or abroad. Continuing with full-time education or training can be a useful alternative if attractive jobs seem scarce, or, for entry to some professions, such as the law or teaching – where a postgraduate qualification is essential if your first degree did not lead to Qualified Teacher Status (QTS). However, you need to be very wary of continuing studying simply because you have found nothing better to do. After all, there is no guarantee that the job market will be any different when you finish postgraduate education – although unemployment among postgrads is very low – and you'll incur even more student debt. But a recent Skills

Task Force survey found that male postgraduates earn up to 20% more than their first-degree peers, whilst for females the figure was up to 34%. This, of course, varies with the level and subject of postgraduate qualification. As always, you need to do your homework about particular courses that interest you.

Off to work?

For many people, the long-term aim of returning to study or training is to be able to put what you have learned to some use. This does not have to be through **paid employment**; there are alternatives.

Certainly, in today's labour market, more people are **self-employed** or work on a freelance basis. An estimated 3.5 million people work for themselves in Britain. Some adult returners use their new skills and qualifications as a springboard to set up their own businesses. Quite a number of people who don't need to increase their income, or who have some flexibility in terms of demands on their time, are able to step off the employment conveyor belt and take up **voluntary work**. If you can't find a suitable job at present, time spent on worthwhile voluntary projects can be a valuable way of demonstrating to future employers your determination and ability to work. In some fields, it can be the only way of getting the experience necessary to enter paid employment or to being accepted onto a training course. Organisations like VSO (Voluntary Service Overseas), which have been traditionally associated with young people, increasingly seek mature, even retired, people with greater experience and a comprehensive range of skills. But don't think that voluntary work is a soft option: the scope varies enormously and may require a special sort of personal commitment.

Employability

If, however, your goal is to find work after a course, or to get a better job, then there are several factors to take into account. Perhaps the most important point to stress is that although learning can be a useful stepping stone to employment with improved prospects, it does not offer any guarantees. Secondly, your choice of course can be a determining factor.

A look at *What do Graduates Do?*, published annually by AgCAS, will give you the different employment and unemployment statistics for different subject areas. For example, in 2002 civil engineering had the highest percentage of students in employment six months after graduation, closely followed by accountancy, business and management studies. Surprisingly, perhaps, (as some commentators regard the subject as one of those 'Mickey Mouse' options) media studies was next on the list.

However, many graduate employers are not so much interested in the subject of an applicant's degree, as by their potential to succeed in the job. Some 60% of graduate vacancies do not specify a particular degree subject. In this context, mature graduates, who present their accumulated skills, qualifications and experience to advantage, may be a step ahead in the employability stakes.

What do employers want?

Although it may take time, it is well worth researching the present and future state of the industry or profession you want to enter, to look at some labour market information, and to understand the specific skills that employers seek. Certainly, recent work experience in the occupational area, gained either:

● from previous employment in that area in an unqualified, or less-qualified, role

● from a placement undertaken during your course

● through vacation or part-time work while you have been studying

● or by working in a voluntary capacity

can be a considerable advantage, as mature learners can demonstrate that they have both commercial understanding and a grasp of modern ways of working in business or industry.

Some people limit their own prospects by concentrating too much on their qualifications rather than on the more general skills that they have acquired. In fact, many employers look for generic, rather than specific, skills. This is particularly true in graduate recruitment, where many employers look at the whole person and not so much at the subject or class of their degree. So, recognise and emphasise your transferable or employability skills. These are the key skills, graduate skills, personal qualities and other attributes – often enhanced by maturity and experience – that can be applied across a variety of work situations. They include the ability to:

- manage and interpret information
- work in pressurised and stressful situations
- communicate clearly and accurately
- work well both alone and in teams
- get on well with other people, including customers, clients and fellow staff
- act ethically.

Don't apologise for your maturity; celebrate it! Mature graduates can often claim to be more adaptable, are likely to commit themselves to one job for longer than a young graduate, and have proved their persistence and motivation just by having been a mature student in the first place. In some occupational areas – like social work, adult education, human resource management, health and community work, guidance and counselling – employers will be looking specifically for people with work experience and maturity. Whatever you do, it will be worth highlighting previous successful work experience, even if it is in areas unrelated to those for which you are applying.

But be aware that graduate employers may believe that older applicants are less willing to move to where the work is, expect higher starting salaries than younger graduates, and often lack the self confidence and self-presentation skills of the young.

Ageism

Perhaps, for many adults, the crucial issue concerns employers' attitudes to the recruitment of older workers and staff. The labour market can be tough on older people and, yet, the prediction is that by the year 2010, almost 40% of the labour force will be aged 45 or older.

The Government is fighting to combat ageism in the workplace through the voluntary *Age Positive* programme – which suggests that employers should think twice before applying age limits to their recruitment and selection procedures and, instead, assess applicants purely on the suitability of their qualifications, skills and experience. In fact, prompted by EU directives, anti-ageism legislation will be introduced in October 2006.

Many companies, who were happy to shed older employees a few years back, have come to agree with the propositions that older workers are more reliable than the young, they bring useful experience to an organisation, and that they are often very keen productive employees with a good attitude to work and 'a lot of mileage left in them'.

Do recognise that you can get help and advice. There are courses, informal support groups, books, websites and self-study packs that cover the spectrum from preparing job applications and writing CVs to practising interview techniques.

Sacha Morris – a mature student second time around

Sacha has retrained as a hospital play specialist and now works at Great Ormond Street Hospital.

'My reason for returning to college was to gain the qualification I needed to carry on my long-term career prospects. This was a bit daunting at first. It had been 12 years since I was a mature student the first time around. My course was only one day a week but quite intense, involving three block weeks. The benefit of this course is receiving a recognised qualification and a sense of achievement.

I felt that returning to college would encourage my own children. If they see me coming home doing college work they will see it as a positive thing and have a better attitude towards their own education.

As the mother of four children ranging from 13 years to 6 years, I have to be very organised. I had full support from my husband and family, which was a great relief. We had to compromise time on the computer and other household duties.

My manager and work colleagues were very supportive. As all the students were mostly in the same position it was easy to bond with everyone in the group and friendships were made very quickly. We are a very close group and all very supportive of each other.

Guilt will be a factor to consider, as you may sometimes feel that the family is being left out, or the housework is not being done. Sometimes there are also worries about being able to keep up to date with the work, which can be stressful and lead to the occasional sleepless night!

But through all this the end result is an enjoyable and stimulating experience and one that I wouldn't hesitate to repeat. I still keep in touch with colleagues from 12 years ago and I hope that I will be able to do the same this time around.

The advice I would pass on to others returning to learning is to be well organised and make a space at home to keep your work together. Be aware children may get sick and other problems that might arise and deal with it the best you can. Keep on top of things in your work and keep to deadlines. Make use of the help you can receive from your colleagues, tutors, friends and family. You can always return a favour at a later date. Above all this enjoy yourself, it may seem never ending at the beginning but believe me time does fly by.'

Further information

Chapter nine lists organisations and agencies that can help you.

Learning providers also offer practical help to their students. Some of this help may be quite informal; for example, tutors can advise on progression routes in their own subject area. Colleges are able to provide careers advice, either through their own student support service or through links with the local adult guidance provider. Every UK university operates a careers service for their own students, staffed by specialists in graduate careers. Recent graduates can seek careers advice from the university nearest home – not necessarily the institution where they studied.

For jobseekers, the local JobcentrePlus or Jobcentre is a first port of call. Their telephone helpline (Employment Direct: 0845 60 60 234) can help you in your search for work. You can be put in touch with recruiting employers and given access to a database of European vacancies – together with the help of a European adviser.

All IAGs and other careers guidance organisations hold useful publications on jobseeking, and usually provide internet access to reach jobseekers' websites.

In searching for work, study the national and local press, professional and trade journals, and the range of weekly appointments magazines that carry national and regional vacancies. These publications are normally held in your local public reference library.

Your local unitary authority should be able to help with information about the labour market in your area, and may offer advice and assistance to people setting up their own businesses.

Other sources of useful information include:

What do Graduates Do?, published by Graduate Prospects/AgCAS, or can be viewed on: www.prospects.ac.uk

The above website also contains useful information for mature students.

For information about setting up your own business, see the Government's Small Business Service website: www.sbs.gov.uk

For information on age discrimination legislation, see: www.agepositive.gov.uk

The JobcentrePlus network also has its own website through which you can access job vacancies: www.jobcentreplus.gov.uk

Labour market information can be found on: www.statistics.gov.uk www.skillsbase.dfes.gov.uk

Chapter nine
Where to get help

'My advice to anyone contemplating enrolling on a course is to find out as much as possible about the course before you commit yourself. Time taken at this stage will help to eliminate the possibility of a bad experience!'

Advice about returning to learning can be found in many places. This chapter focuses on sources of help and advice available to you, and where to find them. If you've made your mind up to return to learning, you will need reliable information and advice before taking your next step. If you still haven't decided whether a return to education or training is for you, or you are unsure of the learning route you want to take, you may need professional guidance. Some of the main sources of help are described below, under the following headings:

- **course providers**

- **educational and careers guidance agencies for adults**

- **Learning and Skills Councils and Local Enterprise Companies**

- **JobcentrePlus/Jobcentres**

- **voluntary agencies, campaigns and charities**

- **professional bodies**.

Organisations covered by the first four headings are primarily local sources of help, providing a service to a particular region or catchment area – although with national links. Under the last two headings, you will find organisations that offer a service for specific

groups of people, or that can provide information about particular careers and industries. So, for example, in the section on voluntary agencies there are details of agencies that can advise women, older people, people with disabilities, ex-offenders and refugees, while the professional bodies cater for would-be engineers, teachers, social workers etc.

Arthur Smith – swapped sausages for statistics

Former butcher Arthur was forced to change careers after developing an illness. He enrolled on an accountancy course.

'I worked in the butchery trade for twenty years after leaving formal education at fifteen without any qualifications. About three years ago I developed a serious, debilitating disease, which affected my muscles. This condition makes it hard for me to walk. I need to use walking sticks and I also find it difficult to climb stairs. Some days I can't cope with driving.

I had to give up butchery but I was determined that this wouldn't stop me from providing for my family. I enquired at my local college, to see what other options were open to me and I enrolled as an accountancy student.

I did have some fears about going back to education but these were eased by my 11-year-old son and by the support of my wife. My son is highly amused to be doing his homework alongside his Dad and that, like me, he also has to get his homework finished and in on time.

As I approached the age of forty, I must admit the thought of going to a college full of youngsters scared me to death. But with the loving bullying from my wife and all the support anyone could ask from the college staff I have overcome any obstacles in my way, I am glad to be able to say.

I have gained many things from my learning experience not just the qualifications I have obtained and hope to gain at college but also the improvement of my self-confidence.

I attend college four days a week and spend another day of unpaid work experience at a local accountancy practice. It would have been easy for me to have just sat at home and sulked but having something to aim for and try to achieve is sometimes the best medicine you can take.

> *I may not be as active as I once was but as one door shuts so another one opens. I thought if I can't use my muscles I will try and use my brain. Learning has given me a new focus, a new structure to my life and set of aims and objectives that I feel I am well on the way to achieving.*
>
> *For all the opportunities, that have been put before me as a result of taking the decision to go back to learning, all I can really say is a big thank you.'*

The course providers

Just as students have a story to tell, so do the people who work in education and training centres, colleges and universities. Staff will be able to tell you in detail about the courses they run, what might be suitable for you and how previous people on the course have fared. Lots of information will be available on their website and in the prospectus, but there are usually questions to which you will want a more personalised answer.

Many adult education centres, colleges and universities are able to provide general educational guidance as well as giving detailed information about the courses they offer. For the most part these services are designed for potential students, but some colleges also provide information about courses offered by other learning providers in their locality.

As well as information about their courses, colleges are well placed to advise on issues such as fees, extra financial help and childcare. They can tell you about entry requirements and how you can get credit for your current skills through accreditation or assessment of your previous learning and experience (APL and APEL).

Try to talk to the right person. While the reception and enquiry desks will be able to deal with many general enquiries, you will need to speak to other staff to get detailed advice and guidance. Ask if the college has anyone who specialises with enquiries and applications from mature students. Otherwise, try the admissions staff, student services unit or advice and guidance centre (or any permutation of these – titles vary). If you are interested in a particular course, ask to speak to one of the course tutors. Even current or previous students may be useful sources of information on a range of important issues, such as 'bring a packed lunch! School dinners have yet to evolve'.

> *'I would give anyone the advice that you should return to studies and, no matter what, get on with your learning rather than push yourself away in the corner and think you're not capable enough to complete or accomplish anything. Research the course that you're interested in and make sure that it's the right one for you. Look where the course might lead you in terms of career or job prospects, and how long your studies will last. Always keep in mind why you're doing the course and that only you can hold yourself back. Once you've decided, go for it and apply.'*

If you have a specific occupational area in mind, but are having difficulty finding a training provider, you can contact that industry's Sector Skills Council (SSC). The Sector Skills Development Agency can help you find the appropriate Sector Skills Council. SSCs are still under development, and many have evolved from, or replaced National Training Organisations (NTOs), which ceased to be recognised by the Government in March 2002. Despite this, some NTOs are still active although they will be gradually phased out as more and more SSCs are approved for licence. It is anticipated that there will be a smaller number of the new Sector Skills Councils, which will have better resources than the previous NTOs.

Sector Skills Development Agency – 3 Callflex Business Park, Golden Smithies Lane, Wath-upon-Dearne, South Yorkshire S63 7ER. Tel: 01709 765444.

You can see more about the Sector Skills Councils existing and in development, on the website: www.ssda.org.uk

Educational and careers guidance services for adults

The quickest way to find out what educational and careers guidance services for adults are available in your area is to ring the learndirect helpline on 0800 100 900 (0808 100 9000 in Scotland). learndirect also provide information on courses, funding and issues such as childcare. Information is also available on the websites: www.learndirect.co.uk and www.learndirectscotland.com

At present, services to adults vary considerably from one area to another. What you get for free, and what you have to pay for, depends on the local service's policy. The Department for Education and Skills provides a national framework and specifications for local information, advice and guidance (IAG) services to adults. IAGs have been developed in England over the last three years, with the aim of helping to widen adult participation in learning and to enhance employability prospects. The network of services on offer in your area is coordinated through an IAG partnership and has to meet national quality standards. Currently each IAG service is locally branded, though it is planned that in the future, IAG services will have a national identity – possibly as the IA Delivery Network.

The service may be provided through various channels in the public, private and voluntary sectors. Examples of these channels include library services, local authorities, Jobcentre Plus as well as more individual projects, set up to target specific issues such as homelessness or drug misuse.

Each IAG provider should have information about the range of educational and training opportunities available in their locality, including basic skills provision. In addition, advisers are available (often by appointment only) to help you make sense of the options – although detailed individual guidance, as stated earlier – may only be available at a price. Information and advice are available on study fees and other costs, and about the availability of financial support. Some centres offer computer-assisted careers guidance, psychometric testing, and careers counselling. Adult guidance services will have links with guidance services for young people, e.g. Connexions; some may share premises. In any case, adults may be able to use the information in services aimed primarily at young people as well as in agencies specifically for adults.

Guidance services should be impartial, confidential and independent.

That means they are not tied to recommending any particular educational institution, training provider or course of action. Government funding only covers the provision of information and advice; professional individual guidance is most likely to be provided as an extra priced service – although disadvantaged groups may be eligible for free guidance.

There is a wealth of information from professional bodies and others, college and university prospectuses and directories and databases are likely to be available for reference, such as:

University and College Entrance: the official guide – published by UCAS.

The Mature Students' Directory – published by Trotman.

What do Graduates Do? – information on graduate destinations available on the 'career centre' section of the Prospects website (in association with AGCAS). www.prospects.ac.uk

The website www.connexions-direct.com/jobs4u is a good starting point for job information. It includes a paragraph on late entry to many careers.

Course Discover – published by Trotman, in association with ECCTIS. A UK-wide database of further and higher education courses.

A useful list of UK-wide contacts, divided into geographical areas, can be found in the Gazetteer section of the DfES publication – *Second Chances* – which may be available for reference in libraries or guidance centres, and can also be viewed on the internet: www.second-chances.uk.com

There are a number of private careers and educational guidance consultancies, which charge fees for advice and guidance. Some are very reputable and offer a comprehensive service. Check whether what they offer could not be obtained cheaper – or even for free – from the Government-funded service, and that their staff are suitably qualified to give guidance and to supervise psychometric tests etc.

In **Northern Ireland**, information is available from your regional Education and Library Boards and the Department for Employment or directly from:

The Educational Guidance Service for Adults (EGSA) – 4th Floor, Linenhall Street, Belfast BT2 8BA. Tel: 028 9024 4274. www.egsa.org.uk

Scotland has an all-age careers service '**Careers Scotland**' set up by the Scottish Executive. They have a comprehensive website and a national number 0845 8502 502. www.careers-scotland.org.uk

In **Wales** there is also a new all-age careers service, '**Careers Wales**' (funded by the Welsh Assembly) which links to seven regional independent companies. www.careerswales.com

The learndirect helpline on 0800 100 900 can put you in touch with your nearest guidance network or education and training provider.

learndirect Scotland has a different number 0800 100 9000 and website: www.learndirectscotland.com

Learning and Skills Councils and Local Enterprise Companies

The LSC funds and plans education and training in England. The LSC is responsible for a network of 47 local offices, and a national office in Coventry, and deals with all post-sixteen education and training, apart from universities. This includes further education, work-based training, workforce development, adult and community learning, IAG services and business links. Your local LSC can tell you about training opportunities in your area.

Look in the telephone directory or contact your local Jobcentre Plus/ Jobcentre for details about the LSC in your area or try the LSC website: www.lsc.gov.uk which lists all the local offices.

In Wales Education and Learning Wales (ELWa) has responsibility for adult continuing education and work based learning for adults.

In Scotland, Training for Work is offered through Local Enterprise Companies (LECs).

In Northern Ireland all training schemes and related initiatives, such as Focus for Work, Worktrack and Training for Work are run by the Department for Employment and Learning.

Jobcentre Plus/Jobcentres

Although primarily a job-finding agency, your local Jobcentre Plus/ Jobcentre will also have printed information and computer databases on education and training opportunities for job-changers. More specifically, it is your major point of contact for information about government-funded training schemes. Jobcentre Plus/Jobcentres can usually find answers to all your queries about job-seeking and benefits available in the one place. The Jobcentre Plus also has a website that has information about benefits and local offices, as well as jobs! www.jobcentreplus.gov.uk

Voluntary agencies, campaigns and charities

Many voluntary agencies and charities are concerned with education and training. In many cases, this concern takes the form of campaigning for better access for particular groups in society. But some agencies are a useful source of additional information and can provide specialist educational guidance and counselling – and sometimes even training provision. Listed here are additional sources of help for women, older people, people with disabilities, ex-offenders, refugees and overseas students.

For women

Campaigns to promote better opportunities for women in education and training operate both at a national and a local level. They can be useful sources of information about education provision. A few organisations that operate nationally are described here.

The Women Returners' Network – WRN, Chelmsford College, Moulsham Street, Chelmsford, Essex CM2 0JQ. Tel: 01245 263796. www.women-returners.co.uk

This organisation works for greater education, training and employment opportunities to help women re-enter the workforce. The network encourages providers of education to develop flexible education and training programmes to meet the needs of women.

Women into Science and Engineering (WISE) – 22 Old Queen Street, London SW1H 9HP. Tel: 020 7227 8421. www.wisecampaign.org.uk

WISE is a campaign to encourage more girls and women to consider careers in science, engineering and technology (SET). An annual directory – entitled *Directory of Initiatives* – listing information on awards, scholarships, courses and family-friendly policies is available as well as posters magazines and videos. All WISE publications are free. The website has a specific section for returners.

WISE initiatives have also been set up in Northern Ireland, Wales and Scotland and details can be accessed via the national website.

Women's Training Network – Northway Centre, Maltfield Road, Marston, Oxford OX3 9RF. Tel: 01865 741317. www.wtn.org.uk

A national non-profit making organisation which promotes vocational training for disadvantaged women in areas of work where women are under-represented – such as construction, IT, electronics etc.

For older learners

The guidance services and most further and higher education programmes featured throughout this book are generally available to anyone regardless of age. Indeed, new legislation against age discrimination in employment and vocational training should be in place by 2006. However, until that time, much purely vocational training will have an upper age limit – even if it is sometimes as high as 60. But the majority of education institutions work on the principle that it is never too late to learn, and educational guidance services should be able to offer good advice to people of all ages. The following are organisations that cater specifically for older people.

NIACE (National Institution of Adult and Continuing Education): The National Organisation for Adult Learning – The Older and Bolder Programme Information Officer, 21 De Montfort Street, Leicester LE1 7GE. Tel: 0116 204 4227. www.niace.org.uk

NIACE works for all adults, but its Older and Bolder programme specifically promotes learning opportunities for people over 50. If you think that's over the hill, some of the regional winners of the Senior Learner of the year 2004 awards were aged 92 and 89. One lady completed a PhD at 87!

'I have simply become a 'cool' up-to-date person, rather than remaining on yesterday's scrap heap' – says one 71-year-old winner

Age Concern – 1268 London Road, London SW16 4ER. Tel: 020 8765 7200 (General Enquiries). Freephone information line 0800 00 99 66. www.ace.org.uk

Age Concern produces a series of factsheets on a range of topics including one entitled *Leisure and Learning*. These are available by phoning the information line, or to download from the website. Age Concern collects information on education and leisure activities for older people. As the first point of contact, get in touch with Age Concern locally. There are some 1400 groups and organisations throughout the country. They should be able to advise you about local opportunities or point you in the right direction.

The University of the Third Age (U3A) – National Office, 19 East Street, Bromley, Kent BR1 1QH. Tel: 020 8466 6139. www.u3a.org.uk

U3A provides an opportunity for older people to share educational, creative and leisure activities. The idea behind the University is to bring education further into the community, providing more opportunities for all older people, not simply to learn but also to teach and share their knowledge and experience with others. Because of this informal style of learning, no qualifications are involved. The University now has around 140,000 members in over 500 local groups. The website contains details of local groups.

Third Age Employment Network – 207-221 Pentonville Road, London, N1 9UZ. Tel: 020 7843 1590. www.taen.co.uk

Through local groups, this organisation pools information on guidance and training as well as employment issues.

For people with disabilities

There are a number of organisations that can provide specialist advice for people with disabilities. Before consulting them, it is worth talking to the educational guidance agencies who may be well informed both about opportunities and about how people with disabilities have fared previously with local education providers. Colleges, adult education centres and universities may be able to help directly. Most have appointed staff with responsibility for coordinating support for disabled people.

It is unlawful to discriminate against a person with a disability with regard to college admissions or the services an institution provides for its students. As a requirement of the Disability Discrimination Act, colleges and universities must, at least, be able to tell you about their facilities and services for students with disabilities. Many providers already go further than the minimum requirement: they will be able to advise on course options, help with transport and access and arrange support for those with particular learning difficulties. The Open University has a specialist adviser for students with disabilities, and a team of volunteers who assist students with disabilities at summer schools.

Information about the Disability Discrimination Act, as well as other relevant information on benefits and other topics of interest can be found can be found on the website: www.disability.gov.uk

Skill (the National Bureau for Students with Disabilities) – Chapter House, 18-20 Crucifix Lane, London SE1 3JW. Tel: 020 7450 0620. Freephone: 020 7657 2337. www.skill.org.uk

Skill campaigns to increase opportunities in education, training and employment for people with disabilities or learning difficulties. The Bureau is concerned with people whose needs arise from physical and sensory disabilities, learning difficulties or mental health problems. Skill operates an information service, which welcomes enquiries by letter or by telephone, and publishes a number of useful information sheets for those wishing to return to education.

RNIB Education and Employment Information Service – RNIB, 105 Judd Street, London WC1H 9NE. Tel: 020 7391 2151. Helpline: 0845 766 9999 (Monday-Friday 9.00 – 5.00pm): www.rnib.org.uk

RNIB Vocational College – Radmoor Road, Loughborough, Leicestershire LE11 3BS. Tel: 01509 611077. www.rnibvocoll.ac.uk

The Royal National Institute for the Blind (RNIB) has a student support service for those in (or planning to be in) further and higher education. RNIB advisers can provide guidance on finance and courses, including provision at RNIB specialist colleges for people with visual impairment. They can advise on the range of specialist equipment available to facilitate study. There are a number of RNIB residential specialist colleges throughout the UK, one of these being the RNIB Vocational College in Loughborough. Students can study a broad range of courses, from specialist vocational courses to courses offered in partnership with Loughborough College, such as NVQs, HNDs and A levels.

RADAR – Unit 12, City Forum, 250 City Road, London EC1V 8AF. Tel: 020 7250 3222 www.radar.org.uk

The Royal Association for Disability and Rehabilitation (RADAR) works for people with disabilities on a range of issues. Organised into local groups – including, of course, disabled people – one of RADAR's aims is to help people with disabilities make informed choices about education.

For ex-offenders

NACRO – 169 Clapham Road, London SW9 0PU. Tel: 020 7582 6500. www.nacro.org.uk

Established in 1966, and currently helping over 25,000 people each year, NACRO is the leading charity working to promote social inclusion, reduce crime and resettle offenders. NACRO runs practical projects for offenders, ex-offenders and other vulnerable people across England and Wales. These include training and employment projects for people in contact with the Criminal Justice System – both in prisons and in the community. The focus of much of this work is on enabling people to gain both vocational and basic skills, such as literacy and communication, in order to live constructive and law-abiding lives. NACRO also works to inform policy, including in the areas of offender employment and special needs education and training.

SACRO – 1 Broughton Market, Edinburgh EH3 6NU.
www.sacro.org.uk

In Scotland there are no comparable educational guidance services for ex-offenders, although SACRO can help in other matters.

NIACRO – 169 Ormeau Road, Belfast BT7 1SQ. Tel: 028 9032 0157. www.niacro.co.uk Although they do not have a dedicated education service, the Northern Ireland Association for the Care and Resettlement of Offenders (NIACRO) can provide information, advice and support to offenders, ex-prisoners and immediate relatives on education matters. NIACRO runs training programmes aimed at enhancing skills and qualifications which enhance employability supported by ESF/New Deal. It also manages the Educational Trust (an independent charity) which supports offenders in accessing education where no other funding is available.

For non-UK nationals

For those from overseas, the main educational and careers guidance services are useful sources of information. Colleges and community education centres are also helpful. Many run ESOL courses (English for speakers of other languages), some in conjunction with educational guidance and careers counselling. In addition to the main guidance agencies, other organisations which offer specialist guidance to refugees and others from overseas are:

Education Action International – Refugee Education and Training Advisory Service (RETAS) – 14 Dufferin Street, London EC1Y 8PD. Tel: 020 7426 5800. www.education-action.org

RETAS is now part of Education Action International. RETAS has information on all aspects of the UK educational system, and can advise on professional requalification and on eligibility to student support and other benefits. The service also offers some specialised training schemes of its own for refugees, such as business start-up and jobsearch courses.

The Refugee Council – Head Office, 240-250 Ferndale Road, London SW9 8BB. Tel: 020 7346 6700. www.refugeecouncil.org.uk

The Council has an education and training centre, and helps refugees and asylum seekers to obtain accreditation of their overseas qualifications as well as offering assistance in obtaining education and training in the UK. They also offer careers advice and guidance service for asylum seekers and refugees.

UK NARIC – Oriel House, Oriel Road, Cheltenham GL50 1XP. Tel: 0870 990 4088. www.naric.org.uk

The UK NARIC (National Academic Recognition Information Centre) helps people to relate their overseas academic qualifications to the British system. The service is free to individuals – unless exceptionally lengthy research is required. A letter of comparability costs £30. Write, enclosing a photocopy of your certificate, with translation if necessary, or fax a copy to 01242 258611.

Professional bodies

There are numerous organisations which can provide careers advice and educational guidance related to specific trades, vocations and professions. These range from professional associations such as the Royal Institute of British Architects to bodies with a responsibility for recruitment such as the Teacher Training Agency. These organisations should at least be able to give general information about the type of qualifications you will need for entry into a particular career at a given point. At best, they might be able to offer more comprehensive advice on prospects, on courses (including those which give exemption to professional exams) and on which colleges and universities have good reputations in the relevant disciplines. Most have websites as well as printed information.

For anybody considering education as a route into a particular career, it is worth trying to find out if there is an appropriate professional body or organisation which covers the profession. For example, if you wish to study to become a photographer and want advice on appropriate courses, then try contacting the British Institute of Professional Photography. Unfortunately, there is no easy way of finding out which organisations can advise about particular careers; arrangements vary from profession to profession. However, the educational and careers guidance services featured earlier in the chapter should be able to help.

In England (despite the fact that the service is not all-age) you may be able to use the resources available at your local Connexions/careers centre libraries to find addresses. Staff will show you how to understand the classification system!

Further information

Local reference libraries will have books and databases on local and national education and training opportunities. Your Citizens Advice Bureau can help you on issues such as entitlement to benefits while studying. Help is also available on the website www.nacab.org.uk 'Quality' newspapers often carry articles about careers, labour market and education issues – watch out for those buzzwords 'lifelong learning'!

Publishers' contact details

This list gives the contact details of publishers referred to in this book (other than those where points of contact are provided within the text). Where appropriate, the telephone number, fax number and email address are given for ordering publications.

City & Guilds – 1 Giltspur Street, London EC1A 9DD. Tel: 020 7294 2800. Fax: 020 7294 2400. Email: equiries@city-and-guilds.co.uk www.city-and-guilds.co.uk

Directory of Social Change – 24 Stephenson Way, London NW1 2DP. Tel: 020 7209 5151. Fax: 020 7391 4804. Email: books@dsc.org.uk www.dsc.org.uk

Graduate Prospects – Prospects House, Booth Street East, Manchester M13 9EP. Tel: 0161 277 5200. Fax: 0161 277 5210. www.prospects.ac.uk

How To Books – 3 Newtec Place, Magdalen Road, Oxford OX4 1RE. Tel: 01865 793806. Email: info@howtobooks.co.uk www.howtobooks.co.uk

ISCO Careerscope – Publications Department, 12A Princess Way, Camberley, Surrey GU15 3SP. Tel: 01276 21188. Fax: 01276 691833. Email: sales@careerscope.info www.careerscope.info

Kogan Page – 120 Pentonville Road, London N1 9JN. Tel orders: 01903 828800. Fax orders: 01903 828801. Email: orders@lbsltd.co.uk www.kogan-page.co.uk

Lifetime Careers Publishing – 7 Ascot Court, White Horse Business Park, Trowbridge BA14 0XA. Tel orders: 01202 665432. Fax orders: 01202 666219. Email: sales@lifetime-publishing.co.uk www.lifetime-publishing.co.uk

NIACE – 21 De Montfort Street, Leicester LE1 7GE. Tel: 0116 204 4216. Email: orders@niace.org.uk www.niace.org.uk

Open University Worldwide Ltd – Michael Young Building, Walton Hall, Milton Keynes MK7 6AA. Tel: 01908 858785. Fax: 01908 858787. Email: ouwenq@open.ac.uk   www.ouw.co.uk

Palgrave Macmillan – Orders, Brunel Road, Houndmills, Basingstoke RG21 6XS. Tel: 01256 302866. Fax: 01256 330688. Email: orders@palgrave.com   www.palgrave.com

Trotman – 2 The Green, Richmond, Surrey TQ9 1PL. Tel orders: 0870 900 2665. Fax orders: 020 8486 1161. Email: orders@trotman.co.uk   www.ordermaster.co.uk

UCAS – UCAS Distribution, PO Box 130, Cheltenham, Gloucestershire GL52 3ZF. Tel: 01242 544610. Fax: 01242 544960. Email: distribution@ucas.ac.uk   www.ucas.com

Index

V

W